Generation without Memory

A JEWISH JOURNEY IN CHRISTIAN AMERICA

ANNE ROIPHE

SUMMIT BOOKS

NEW YORK LONDON TORONTO SYDNEY TOKYO

SUMMIT BOOKS
Simon & Schuster Building
Rockefeller Center
1230 Avenue of the Americas
New York, New York 10020

First Summit trade paperback, 1989
SUMMIT BOOKS and colophon are
trademarks of Simon & Schuster Inc.
Designed by Eve Metz
Manufactured in the United States of America

10 9 8 7 6 5 4 3 2 1

Library of Congress Cataloging-in-Publication Data

Roiphe, Anne Richardson, date
  Generation without memory.

    1. Judaism—United States.   2. Jews—United States—
Cultural assimilation.   3. Jews—United States—Identify.
4. Roiphe, Anne Richardson, date   —Religion.
5. Novelists, American—20th century—Biography.
6. Roiphe, Anne Richardson, date   —Biography.
I. Title.
[BM205.R56   1989   973'.04924   89-11450
ISBN 0-671-69001-9

The author gratefully acknowledges permission to quote from the following:
THE TEMPTATION TO EXIST by E. M. Cioran, © 1968 by Quadrangle/The
New York Times Book Company;
"Address to the Society of B'nai B'rith," from THE STANDARD EDITION
OF THE COMPLETE PSYCHOLOGICAL WORKS OF SIGMUND FREUD, vol-
ume 20, translated and edited by James Strachey, © 1959 by The Hogarth
Press Ltd., Sigmund Freud Copyrights Ltd., and The Institute of Psycho-
Analysis;
JUDAISM IN THE SECULAR WORLD by Jacob Neusner, KTAV Publishing
House, © 1970 by Jacob Neusner.

My brother, Dr. Eugene Roth, Jr., shared with me some of his knowledge and all of his sense of the ridiculous—for that I am thankful. I wish also to acknowledge the gifts of time and thought of Rabbi Paul Steinberg of the Hebrew Union College of New York and Francine Klagsbrun, author of *Voices of Wisdom*.

FOR MY STEPDAUGHTER, JEAN

January 1, 1980

Four o'clock in the afternoon of New Year's Day. The winter sun, a silver disc, cold like the eye of God, slides rapidly toward the bare hills on the far side of the Shepaug River. The sky is mottled gray—an echo of the stone fences in the nearby fields. Above the white cupola of the Congregational church heavy snow clouds float—borne by the sharp winds blowing from the north. The bare trees sway (black lines etched in the frigid air, twigs, branches, fallen logs, some catching the sharp light of the fading sun, shine like the swords of young armies). Over the slope just before the village green, a clump of old elms leans into the shadows, twisted, curled, waiting for further darkness to hide their sterility.

As we drive up to the green the church doors open. A single candle light begins to shine in each of the perfect, equidistant rectangular windows on the first and second floors. We can see the pure mahogany rail of the balcony, the white cloth of the altar and the rows of simple pine seats. The white clapboard Colonial church with black shutters stands (its light at each window) with a grace that reflects the long-dead architect's knowledge of proportion, of distance of pillar from frame, of height and width. His Yankee Puritan intuition of order and limitation had created, nearly two hundred years ago, this brave assertion of the human gathering. The small steady lights at each of the windows refuse the evening sky and answer back with a quiet pride of their own. A child runs out and bends over the fir tree near the white steps of the church. Small blue lights suddenly appear in the tree and over

9

by the drugstore a multicolored Christmas wreath starts shimmering red and gold. Tiny white bulbs begin to blink on the second floor of the parsonage where an old, bedridden woman has celebrated the holiday. Cars have lined up along the road near the shuttered doors of the post office. Families, babies in buntings, children in down jackets and party shoes, women with sprigs of plastic holly pinned to their wool coats, are entering the church. Some kind of New Year's celebration is about to begin.

I turn my car around. My children are staring out the window at the church. They are silent. As our nameless and forgotten recent forebears stood in their villages of the Ukraine and Lithuania looking at the village church, so too are we aliens, outsiders in a Christian world where the symbols of redemption, resurrection and holiness are to us only images, words, lights that beckon others, promises that build a circle of faith, or perhaps only a circle of hands, of people who will call each other brethren and share certain stories in a way so effortless as to make them all kin while we as always are strangers, newcomers, wanderers. The sweet lights in the church are like a campfire keeping away the wild beasts of imagination if not of reality. We cannot move toward that campfire. We cannot warm our feet or hands there, because we are Jews. Or are we still Jews? Do we dare call ourselves Jews? Do we dare not call ourselves Jews? My grandfather Isaac who came to this country when he was nine and took up his pushcart when he was ten and started a shirt factory when he was twenty and at thirty-five sent his wife to Europe to purchase fine lace tablecloths and silver and dishes for their new home on Riverside Drive . . . my grandfather Isaac who gave his two sons his business and saw two of his daughters well married, he did not have time to ask the question. He did not belong to a time when the question could be asked.

Perhaps history moves like a snake devouring its own tail . . . perhaps it moves like a belly dancer: teasing us, hypnotizing us with promises of satisfactions always postponed till the houselights go dark and the waiter takes off his white coat and there's nothing to do with the evening's expectations but take them home to sleep. Circular or linear, history has carried us away from the shtetls of Russia and Rumania, Poland and Hungary. We were driven or we drifted onto the Lower East Side, out to the fringes of Flatbush and onto the streets of the Western world, to medical school, to condominiums in Boca Raton, to suburbs and exurbs. As a family we moved from the eleventh century to the twentieth in two generations. The speed has been dazzling. We are shaking like astronauts passing through dimensions of space and sound. We are in Hannah Arendt's terms "parvenu." We are also "nouveau." We are in Sartre's terms "nonauthentic." We have escaped the night of ignorance, of superstition, of poverty, of the narrow streets of the Old World where science and technology had been beyond all reach. Our particular relatives having been desperate or hopeful enough, we escaped the Holocaust. It is always quite clear to us how close we came to providing additional material evidence of Jehovah's grand indifference to man and man's unsurpassed cruelty. We escaped, but along the way we lost comforts, consolations, communities. We escaped, but we are more alone than ever before. Are we still Jews? Dare we call ourselves Jews? Dare we not? Is it possible to be without a name? Are we brave enough or foolish enough to try?

Islam runs riot in the streets. Each fist raised, each back raw from self-flagellation, each Ayatollah, each woman demure in her chador speaks of a unity, of a belonging, of a person with an individual name but a sense of himself or herself as part of a collective. A Moslem living in the Moslem universe, a fleck, a dot, a molecule, but nevertheless a part of the whole. In storefronts in Harlem, on hilltops and back streets of the South and in the West, born-again Christians speak in tongues. Episcopalians and Methodists hold church fairs and bake sales. The historian Will Durant, now himself an ancient man, has said the world is turning in a conservative leap back toward totalitarian religious controls, to a time when the individual was subordinate to the community ethic and ritual. In the synagogues the remnant, the Orthodox Jews, still pray each morning (still thanking God for not having made them female), and the holy words of the Torah, the religious work goes on season after season and under the fringed tallis black coats are rocking back and forth in assured piety. In suburbs Jewish sons and daughters are Bar Mitzvahed and Bas Mitzvahed and Catholic communicants in white dresses carrying small bouquets of flowers mark their entry into their religions. Families of both groups celebrate at Holiday Inns conveniently located near highways and shopping centers.

Our family has no house of worship and we don't send our children to Sunday school. Can we get away with this arrogance or do we pay too high a price for our independence? Are we still Jews? Do we dare not be Jews?

My daughter Katie is now eleven. Her best friend for the last five years has also been named Kate. The other Kate has thin, blond, straight hair and she stands several inches taller than our Kate. In her strong arms she sweeps my child in constant hugs in the passionate clasp of deep childhood love. The other Kate's eyes are blue and like her mother she keeps all her facts straight. She reads biographies of kings and queens and presidents. The bright, quick, gifted energy of her mind reaches eagerly out to new math concepts and geography patterns. When she comes into the room we all smile. She seems so clean, so clear, so purposeful and direct. She breathes out the Protestant ethic, a diligence, an energy, a fierce intelligent certainty that tomorrow will be an improvement over today and if there are difficulties they will be solved. She is not expecting dislocations or abrupt changes. She is like the Hans that

Thomas Mann's Tonio Kröger admired so much; she is the light and the fair, the secure and the well-centered.

· Neither my husband nor I, although we grew up in different economic worlds, had any Christian friends when we were children. Our Kate is in the first generation of our family not to have been raised in a ghetto of one sort or another. The other Kate's grandfather is an Episcopal minister and often on Sunday her mother, in a dress and pearls, handbag and stockings, goes off to church. She graduated from Harvard Law School and during the week works in New York. Sundays she teaches the Bible class at St. Andrew's Church in Connecticut. The other Kate brings us gingerbread cookies for our tree every Christmas. Her socks are always slipping down inside her Docksiders. Her cheeks are always pink and when she throws a ball it really goes hard and far. She and her dad frequently go to Yankee baseball games. Sometimes they take our Kate, who tries to care but her mind wanders. Our Kate has thick curly hair. Under her eyes she has circles that deepen as the day goes on and sometimes when she's not feeling well they turn violet against her pale skin. She has brown eyes that sometimes look so sad I wonder if they belong to someone else, someone older, perhaps, who had seen for herself the unimaginable. Our Kate loves Dickens and Gothic romances. A year ago she read *The Diary of Anne Frank* and after that other books on refugee childhoods, on the bombing of England, on the internment of the Japanese in California, on the massacre of the Armenians. She won't talk to me about what she has read. Silently she returns the books to the library and comes back with more. Our Kate looks at the world with that peculiar inborn woe of the East European. Not all our children are like this, some are riders of the surf and rock singers, but this one seems to have a nest of violins and cows and bouquets of flowers floating over her head. Is she Chagall's child or ours?

Our Kate does not believe in life after death. Our Kate does not believe in Christian charity (reports of pogroms have caused her to regard Easter as more than a matter of bunnies

and jelly beans). We have told her that we are Jewish because our parents were but that we don't go to a synagogue
because we don't believe in ritual. We are humanists, I explained, although we don't expect too much of humanity. We
are agnostics, I explained. My child has many questions I
can't answer. She is already more burdened than the other
Kate. Is that because she is Jewish? Or is she Jewish? Dare she
not be? Is she, trick or treating for UNICEF, tribeless and
clanless? Is she weighted down with a freedom beyond en-
durance? Will she join the Moonies, the Hare Krishnas, the
Weatherpeople, or the 1990 versions of the same? Is it possible that alienation like leukemia can carry off the young? I
watch the two Kates through my window. The other Kate
jumps over the rocks and the ice rivulets that crisscross our
field. My Kate walks cautiously. She doesn't like the wind and
she covers her ears with her hands. "Wait," she calls to her
friend who is now far ahead. Her friend turns around and
waits.

After Napoleon, as the Enlightenment spread over Europe,
Jews entered the Western world creating new wrinkles in "the
Jewish problem" wherever they went. Some made money.
Some achieved secular education—none could dissolve the tu-
mor of anti-Semitism that grew in the gut of modern Europe.
We know who had the last bitter laugh. Is anti-Semitism inevitable, natural like the rain and the moss? Will it die down
only to reappear stronger and more virulent than ever? "In
each generation, it will come again," says a psychoanalyst friend
of mine. "We must teach the children to be prepared. In each
generation someone will attempt to annihilate the Jews." They
are bombing synagogues in Europe and painting swastikas in
Great Neck. They are gathering again. Do I believe that? Is
history circular or linear? Is it safe to believe that we are safe?

My mother, the youngest of five, was playing under the kitchen table—the year must have been 1914. Her aunts, her father's sisters, were preparing dinner. In the midst of their conversation they spoke the family name. The name they had used in Poland. The name that had been changed to Phillips some time after their appearance before the immigration officer at Ellis Island. There was a sound of a toy rolling across the floor. They dragged her out. Raging and weeping and calling to God in a steady stream of Yiddish, they jumped on her. One aunt pinched the child's arm until the child too was crying. One of the aunts shouted, "If you ever tell anyone the name you heard, your children and your children's children will be cursed with disease and pain, misfortune and early death. If you tell this secret to any of your older sisters or brothers, their children too will die in agony. Not a soul must know the name of our family before we came to America." The aunts allowed the little child to make her escape and returned to the cutting and the peeling and the chopping—the preparations for a meal that my still frightened mother was unable to share.

My mother told me that story when I was a child. "Tell me the name," I begged her. "I won't tell anyone," I promised.

"No," she said, "I can't."

I asked my uncles and my aunts and they said they didn't know of any other name. (Perhaps the family had always been called Phillips or Phillipovska.) "Who cares," they said. "Forget about it," they cautioned.

In 1962 when my mother was dying and she knew she was dying, although everyone was promising her health and long life, I sat at the edge of her bed. My baby daughter was playing with her grandmother's jewelry box; strings of pearls, gold bracelets, charms and earrings were rolling about the carpet.

"Please," I said, "now tell me the real family name. If you don't tell me perhaps no one will ever know."

"I can't," she answered, and it was a great effort for her to talk. "I don't want to curse you or the baby."

"You don't believe that," I said. "That's superstition, primitive, childish, magic-ghetto whisperings." I had recently finished college and I thought I knew fact from fiction.

"No," she insisted, "I would bring down the curse on you and your children."

I felt an ancient shadow in the room, a creeping darkness that contained more than just approaching death. Curiosity was stronger than fear.

"Please," I said, "write it out on a piece of paper."

She turned her head away from me and closed her eyes.

Imps and demons of the ghetto, Lilith and Samuel were cheated that day. Phillips was the family name and the family history started at Ellis Island. Lately I have been wondering if not knowing the real name was not a form of curse too. What was the family shame? What was the terrible secret? Was it nothing more than being Jewish and foreign? Or was it perhaps some criminal act that had been committed on the distant ground and covered by a hasty flight to the New World, across an ocean that forgave the old sins in anticipation of the new? Was it perhaps some paranoid belief that the czar's army could reach over the waves and recall its deserters, its impressed servants, and reclaim lives that had been thought free? Or was this wiping out of the name simply an expression of eagerness to become American, to undo the greenhorn condition, to forget what humiliations had been and enter a new world, with a clean slate, where one need not follow in one's father's footsteps and one might redeem the promises of a somewhat silent and unbending Deity.

There are four separate questions that I ask. It is hard to keep them separate since they wind so thickly and easily around each other. Yet for clarity's sake, for the sake of reason, they must be separated.

The first question is purely theological. Do I think God is there? If I accept Him, how does He answer for His crimes? Do I think God is an invention to comfort man on his arduous way through the abyss of chemistry and physics we call universe and time? Baruch Atoh, Adenoi Elohenu . . . yes or no?

The second question is the Jewish one. There is a collective destiny, a historical experience that is Judaism but I, you, we, they do or do not choose to be a part of it. One can be a Jewish atheist, a Jewish Socialist, a Jewish Zionist, a Jewish farmer without believing in the Jewish God. The odd and special part of the Jewish experience is just this nationhood that existed without nation—this sense of historical purpose that is moving forward in some mysterious but necessary condition. Do I, do you, do we choose to be one of this unit, or do I, you, we escape, identifying ourselves only as members of mankind, humans among humans? A second part of this question is the relationship of the Jews of the Diaspora to Israel. If Israel is the redemption of the Jewish people, God's sign after the Holocaust, then if one is connected to the Jewish experience, one must be connected to Israel—but how and to what degree and what is asked and what can be given?

The third question is political. Do I, does anyone, have a choice? Will Jewishness, Yiddishkeit, Jewish culture, be permitted to disappear, and to evaporate in the continued dilutions of intermarriage and assimilation, or will the hostile world once again reject what it had so recently absorbed? The accuracy on thinking about question number three will affect the wisdom of one's final choice on question number two.

The fourth question, and there must be four questions for tradition's sake, in honor of those who first came forth from Egypt and whose story is or is not ours, is to ask if one leaves

the tight world of one's ancestors, if one abandons the synagogue, the High Holy Days, the Sabbath Queen, the Torah,
the Talmud, the Midrash, what replacements are made in the
building of the soul? How are the crises of life marked:
birth, marriage, death? How are festivals managed? Men and
women need ways of living within ethical frameworks, ways
of passing on to their children their morality and their life-
styles. What do we do—we who once thought only of abandoning the ways of our parents and parents' parents and gave
no heed to the necessary replacements, substitutes, we would
need to make—what do we in our empty apartments do to
make furniture and fabric for ourselves?

I have suddenly seen the necessity of question number five.
There should only be four questions to fit the tradition, but
it's so hard to bend the mind to fit within the lines of others
. . . to squeeze and push, to mold one's thinking so that it
neatly suits the designs of the past. I just can't avoid the inex-
actness of asking question number five. Is it possible for a
twentieth-century female, educated to have hopes of equality
and justice, to accept the traditions of a past that have left her
excluded from the law and prevented her from entering the
sacred or the Halakah—how can a feminist feel about the
Jewish religion?

These few questions are asked not to anger those who have
already found their private answers but to permit exploration
of this sensitive subject of assimilation, to allow the spiritual
search to go on as it must. The search for group, for community, for self-knowledge is unending, under constant review. The answers that were comfortable at one period of life
may become hollow at another. One time in history it appears one way and later perhaps another. Tolerance of the
quest is asked.

I know a woman whose Jewish family became wealthy in business. She was sent to a fine girls' school in New York and went on to Smith College. Her Christian boyfriend, who like his father and grandfather had a collection of athletic trophies from the same prep school, was surprised when he entered her apartment in New York and found the closet stuffed with shopping bags.

"But I told you," she said, "my family business is paper bags."

"Oh," he answered, "I thought you said paperbacks—I thought your family was in publishing."

They married and lived happily ever after. They have a house in Connecticut where their children play on the local ice hockey teams and compete in the tennis tournaments. Sometimes she must look up in the sky and think about the devious circles the crow would have to fly to find its way from her mother's childhood in the Bronx to her children's space. And what is she but the agent of transition?

In the forties, on the High Holidays I went as a child with my mother and my brother to the Park Avenue Synagogue. I always had a new outfit for Rosh Hashanah. The holiday always came in the midst of an Indian summer and in the heat one could smell things decaying. We were always standing on the steps of the temple in that moment of stillness just before the coming of the crisp new fall. I would be uncomfortable in my new wool dress and self-conscious in a hat that gave me the appearance of a dwarfed adult. This Conservative congregation was more than prosperous—the businessmen and lawyers and doctors wore blue suits and gray fedoras and silk shirts. Their wives had long red nails, high heels, and even in the heat many of them had their furs draped around their fashionably padded shoulders. My mother wore her fox stole and a hat with a veil that kept getting caught in the frames of her glasses. When my mind wandered from the Hebrew I would fondle the little paws and the soft tail of the fox that she had placed on the pew between us. I was told that the New Year celebration had begun in the year 536 B.C.E. when the convoys of exiles crossed the desert returning from Babylonia to sweep away the broken bricks in the temple courtyard and begin again as a nation at home. In the green hills of Babylonia they had not been altogether miserable. Many decided to stay and others brought back to Judea some seven thousand slaves. In the ancient world the cry "Let my people go" always referred to one particular tribe—not to peoples in general.

In the early evening as the sun was setting over the Hudson River and the buildings along Park Avenue took on the look of pink salmon on golden plates, we left the temple in family clusters—bunches of good burghers for whom the shtetl and its grinding poverty were but shadows in yesterday's dreams. After temple we walked along Park Avenue to my aunt's house, where the crystal and the china and the silver were laid out on the table, offering a promise of permanence even a child could experience. In my aunt's special closet were dishes from France, from England, nineteenth-century Spode, Limoges, Wedgwood. While the grown-ups talked, sometimes the second maid would open the closet door for me and take out one of each set of the rare china. I would sigh as people do at fireworks, each design seeming more miraculous than the one before.

"Happy New Year," everyone said in English.

"Gut Yontiff," they said as they took off their coats. The Czech cook and the Irish maids served the dinner.

"Happy New Year," we said later while standing in the hallway. "Happy New Year," we said, united by the holiday spirit—forgetting for the moment the dislikes and distrusts of the assembled for each other. There was always an orgy of kissing as we stood packed in the downward-floating elevator.

In my mother's family most of the men looked alike. They

grew bald very young and had a history of heart attacks and premature deaths. They had soft, sad eyes and a kind of sallow roundness. They were not athletes or animal lovers. They tended to be quieter than the women, and while they played golf and bridge and read *The Wall Street Journal*, it wasn't so easy to tell what they really cared about at all. They had certain frights caused by the Depression, they had other terrors caused by the war, they had nightmares that owed their origins to no known causes. When two of my uncles smiled, they seemed to choke—to deprecate the smile as a foolish gesture in a bitter world. They took it back before you had received it. Eventually they were unkind to each other's sons.

When I was a child I loved the rabbi's voice and I loved the cantor and I loved the sound of the shofar. I felt in the synagogue a community that made my loneliness no longer mine alone. I was prepared to love YHWH, whose name was not taken in vain, who could appear in the burning bush, who had saved Isaac and commanded Abraham and had parted the Red Sea and gave Esther courage and Judith her power and Jacob his angel. I was hopeful on Yom Kippur when God moved from His seat of judgment to His seat of mercy. I loved God then and the universe He had created in six days and six nights. I feared God dimly and trusted Him more. Why not? I was a child.

While we were in the temple my father went for long walks. He couldn't sit through the service. It was not only a matter of faith—he was a man too restless to sit so long. He would never give himself over to the words of others even if those others were the Almighty or his representatives. He would not be vulnerable to the entreaties of God, nor man, woman nor child. He was clean and handsome, tall and lean. He was self-sufficient. I prayed to God to help him love my mother. I also prayed for peace, victory for the Allies, an end to poverty, and justice for the Negroes. I can hardly remember the synagogue now. There was a stained-glass window with blue and red tones. There was the white satin that covered the inside of the Ark, the gold tassels on the ends of the Torah scrolls, the seats given in memory of Rosenbergs, Goldbergs, of Bernsteins and Schwartzes. Baruch Atoh, Adenoi Elohenu. I did. In Sunday school I listened to all the tales both mythical and historical and fused them into a long story that could have no ending. I colored pictures in the Jewish magazine *The World Over*, and I sent them a poem. My poem was a love song to David who had slain Goliath. After a while I knew enough of Jewish history to be as alarmed about what was to come as I was appalled by what had happened.

At Purim I dressed up as Esther and went to a party. We ate hamantashen (prune cakes in the shape of the villain's hat) and made crackling sounds with noisemakers to mock the evil Haman. There was a parade and the prettiest Esther was chosen. Esther had the opportunity to save the Jewish people because she was beautiful. I too yearned to save my people by offering my body to a king—so was ambition born.

In the basement of the synagogue where the Sunday-school classes were held I had some troubles with my peers. They didn't like it that I always had read the homework and that I raised my hand insistently. In the basement of the synagogue I learned that the law was for men, women were supposed to take care of the house and the children, and that it wasn't too smart for a girl to be too smart. I discovered that women were excluded from the minyan (the ten men required to begin services), from the daily observances, from the sacred obligations, from the honors of the congregation, from the handling of the Torah itself. All the talk about the woman's importance in the home, the bringing of the Sabbath Queen, I dimly recognized as the sugar candies on the gingerbread house of misogyny. In the basement of the synagogue I began to lose my interest, and my theological passions turned instead to secular matters.

Now when the fall comes and the children have just started back to school I find myself whispering to no one in particular, "Happy New Year." I find myself in a new outfit and I remember my mother who said Kaddish for her mother, Yisgadal v'yiskadash; I remember her standing in the temple mourning in a way that I would never be able to do for her. Her mascara would run down her cheeks and she remembered whatever she remembered. Afterward as the rabbi went on with the prayers and the pages of the book grew heavier and heavier on the right side, I would lean over to her and touch her hand. She would reapply her lipstick and straighten her veil.

In my Jewish family there were no Socialists, no anarchists, no supporters of Sacco and Vanzetti, no philosopher kings, no intellectuals, no scholars of renown, no professors of math (my mother thought professors earned too low a salary to be respected anyway), definitely no Communists. They were all business people. They supported the synagogue. They paid their tithe to the Federation of Jewish Philanthropies of New York. They were not overly curious about art or science. In my young adulthood I was ashamed of their opulence and their ignorance, their indifference to the economic conditions of the poor in Harlem, the whites in Detroit. Now, somehow, since my own imperfections have surfaced and announced themselves, I have grown to respect the money they made and to understand the limitations of education and empathy that went with it. They were only human after all, just a generation away from real poverty and pariah status. They enjoyed their comforts and ended in condominiums in Florida. Many more of us in my generation could make choices, received better educations, took for granted opportunities, health care and servants. I would have preferred to have more pride in my genetic past and I would have liked to have claimed as forefathers a Barondess, a Meyer London, Abraham Cahan, Meyer Cohen, some Adlers or Soyers. I would have preferred to come from people who had been part of the Workmen's Circle or the Young Socialists or the followers of Emma Goldman, but this is America and I can only blame myself if my contribution is less than I would have hoped.

The Havdalah prayer marks the end of the Sabbath in the Orthodox home. Sung over a braided candle, the Havdalah welcomes the return of the work week and signals the turning toward the secular world. These are the last words of the prayer: "May our Lord multiply our seed and silver like the sands of the sea and the stars of the night."

In America this particular prayer has been granted. The problem is that as the silver increased it became more and more difficult to return at the end of the work week to the sacredness of the Sabbath. There has been a long association in the galut (the condition of Jewish exile, after the second destruction of the Temple in Jerusalem) between poverty and piety. In English it's alliterative, in Yiddish it may be something more than coincidental.

My brother explains to me that in Hebrew poetry the theme is always repeated in different images (sand and stars); in English we may use rhyme. In Hebrew the reader becomes a fly around which webs of meaning are strung.

Hannah Arendt has written that the small Jewish moneyed class kept the Jewish population in a condition of powerlessness. She believed that the system of charity that permitted the Jews of the shtetl to survive also kept them from becoming a political class-conscious body, rebelling against forces of oppression from the outside. She felt that the Jewish charity network kept many Jews as shnorrers while permitting a few to rise high above the rest. This is, I suppose, a Marxist world view. The Federation dances that I went to . . . the New Year's Eve party at the home of a member of the Lehman family, certainly marked stratifications in Jewish society. These social distinctions, known to all the young denizens of the Viola Wolf dancing class (where some Jewish society sent

24

their children to learn the fox-trot), seem to be mere echoes of the larger Christian stratifications, imitations, not the genuine article. Why shouldn't Jews be as snobbish as anyone else? But perhaps Hannah Arendt is right—the class system within the ghetto did not promote survival. It may have weakened the poor and conditioned them to impotence.

In the shtetl there had been two different paths to social prestige and self-esteem. Money, success in business, the joy of possessions and all the respect that follows, the ability to give charity to others, that was one way. The other, the path of piety or scholarship, was revered by the entire Jewish community, or so all the books do say. After the second destruction of the Temple the scholars became the leaders of the Jewish nation. They kept the community together long after the warriors had all been killed and the conventional weapons to achieve statehood had been proved useless. They created a nation that could persist without sovereignty, and to this particular fact does Judaism earn its respect for learning, its bookish quality, its smarts.

Despite myself I look at the names of the winners of science prizes and observe with pleasure how many are Jewish. I feel a little shabby increasing my own self-esteem by the hard work of others. I laugh at myself. I make ironic remarks and remind myself of my incapacity in algebra. I check the names anyway.

Where does it come from, this sense of being a Jew? For the Orthodox that is an unanswerable question. It is in every waking moment of their lives. It is as much a part of their being as their body, their gender, their parents. I asked the question of Blu Greenberg, professor of religion, chairperson of the Federation-sponsored task force on Jewish women.

"How can I answer that question? Everything in my life

has always been connected to my Jewishness. For me being Jewish is the same as being alive. They're inseparable."

All right, fair enough, but for the rest of us whose upbringing has been more assimilated, less religious or exclusive, the Sunday school was the teacher, the creator of the Jewish imprint.

They taught us in the Sunday school all the vagaries of anti-Semitism. They taught history as if the Jews were the innocent lambs whom God was continually sacrificing as He unfolded some holy plan beyond human imagining. They taught this history to young children who had no other knowledge or framework for the ancient, medieval or modern world. They taught history as if the conflict between Jew and Gentile were the only dramas of note. The assumption was made that all that occurred in human time happened because of the Jews or to the Jews. This early intense indoctrination is of the profoundest importance in how Jews think and feel for the rest of their lives. The tragic events taught as the only historical and religious reality accumulate power and force the closing of the tribal gates to those outside.

(I use the word "tribal" not to conjure up images of barbarians in the dark bush but to refer to the basic unit of human social organization. Civilizations will develop rich layers of art, music, thought, ethics and commerce and still their skeletal structures, their patterns of need satisfying forms, remain the same. I use the word "tribe" to speak of people who share the same basic forms, who share a history and a culture. It is an important word because it reminds us that we are all human beings facing the same challenges from the natural environment and the psychological one. The word "tribe" is an anthropological and sociological word. It evokes the shape of human relationships. It does not preclude the differences between groups or deny the varying levels of civilized accomplishment. It does not diminish us.)

If history is always seen as the struggle between the valiant and good David against the brutish and huge Goliath, then one forgets that Goliath has a story too and his people mourn him also. History learned years later in high school and college never again has the compelling immediacy of the black and white early tales—history with causality, economic forces, nationalism, accident of geography, never has the connected, connecting message of those early lessons in moral and political suffering. Even today if I open my mail and read reports from Amnesty International on torture in Chile, Argentina or Iran, I think instantly of the Spanish Inquisition.

In the Christian Sunday school the children learn the Scriptures. They tell a story of one terrible, religious, mythical act of violence. In the Jewish religious schools the children learn not of one symbolic tragedy (the Crucifixion) with its built-in immediate redemption, but of actual tragedies, hundreds of thousands of them in each era and in every country. Belief in the coming of the Messiah, the redemption, requires the deepest of faiths and the most monumental of trusts. It is a real struggle for a child who has learned history—understood history in his/her gut—as a directed, determined, deliberate persecution of Jews over all the centuries to reconceive, or take seriously, the broader, more general human curves. Taking a new measure of history, a relearning of the basic ingredients, is essential to the assimilation process and explains why assimilation is always only partial, a matter of degree. Once taught Jewish history the pictures never disappear or lose their childhood vividness.

They didn't teach us in Sunday school what every one of us in the Park Avenue Synagogue somehow knew. The German Jews, many of whom had emigrated to America in the early or middle 1800s, looked down on the newer and less well as-

similated arrivals who came from the East. The membership
lists in the country clubs in Westchester where the men played
golf and the women rattled mah-jongg cubes by the poolside
reveal this social history quite clearly. These clubs were
formed first as a place for the German Jews who were excluded from the Christian social arenas, and then other clubs
were formed for the Russian Jews who were in turn excluded
from the German Jewish clubs, and a third set of clubs then
formed for the still newer arrivals whose manners were
thought to be as raw as their entry into the twentieth century.

Jews imitated Christians and began to dislike themselves
on a sliding scale of how Jewish they appeared—how fast they
were to mimic the manners and customs of the majority—
how fast their accent faded and their new tones matched the
American high notes. I have long-nosed cousins who rushed to
plastic surgeons to have their faces Anglicized. My mother and
my aunts told me frequently how lucky I was to have a "good
nose"—a nose that would permit a person to move around in
America in disguise.

"Thank God," my mother said when my baby was only a few
hours old, "thank God, the baby doesn't have my nose. She
has a good nose."

The other day a friend of mine who sends her children to
Temple Emanu-El Sunday school in New York and plans a
summer trip to Israel said, "I don't like those Polish-Jewish
rat faces, do you? I mean those skinny faces with the long
noses and the sunken eyes. I think they're ugly." Her aesthetic
is American. The ideal is a Dallas Cowboy cheerleader. Self-
respect is no easy matter in a melting pot and homogenization
without shame is impossible. Assimilation by definition involved some self-hate, some hatred of others who reminded the
self of where the self had been and might still be. Assimilation
required or at least seemed to require a feeling of superiority to
those who were further behind. The emotional price of self-
loathing has always been high.

My father came to America when he was six. He came from a town in the hills near Bratislava, in the town of Tornova that was sometimes in Hungary and sometimes within the borders of the Austro-Hungarian Empire. In this town there was a lumber mill and his father was the secretary to the count who owned everything in the area. His father could read and write German so he was far better off than the other Jews in nearby villages. Nevertheless, my grandfather was afraid that as a Jew he might lose his job at any moment and he came with his young family to America. My father claims now to understand scarcely a word of Hungarian, German or Yiddish. He's an American, that's all. His mother never really learned English very well and it seems likely that eventually she had to talk to her Americanized children in sign language. My father became such an American that even John Quincy Adams would not have suspected that he had in truth been born on the other side.

My father, a graduate of Columbia Law School, has an attaché case of the softest brown leather. He has shirts with his monogram on them and a cashmere coat with a wine-colored silk scarf. But his sister—the one my mother didn't want in the house—his sister, the one my father would never have introduced to his colleagues or his associates, and whom even my brother and I have only met on two or three occasions, his sister Bea married a jeweler who worked in a small jewelry shop on Queens Boulevard and went to the Catskills for her vacations and belonged to her local synagogue and took rhumba lessons from Arthur Murray and won contests at the sisterhood dances. Despite her enormous size she tiptoed lightly on the dance floors of many a resort and became well-known on the rhumba circuit. She spoke with an accent that reeked of the streets of New York and contained Yiddish translations and dialect fragments that embarrassed my mother and, I suspect, horrified her elegant brother. But after all she was only a girl and no one had pushed her to get an education—what money and ambition there were had been saved for the boys. My father helped her son go to law school. He gave her money when her husband failed in his little business, but he hardly ever invited her to dinner. Ah, well!

My father too was the victim of his own assimilation. My father had to pay a high price for his drive to be successful. In his scramble for money and social status and all the pieces of furniture that marked him off from those at the bottom, he was cut off from his past—amputated from the memories of a more proletarian childhood. He had violent migraine headaches. He had waves of irrational anger that came upon him like storms in the tropics, leaving us all battered and exhausted. He forgot (as he forgot his babyhood language) how to look at a woman, a child, a friend. He forgot how to admit fear. He could not comfort and he could not be comforted. He became so American that he was like a pioneer, a trapper in a distant forest of his own making. Silent as a Yankee, his urban world required that he learn to move like a tiger, to trust no one, to need no one. He has told me very few things about his childhood—a veil of secrecy lies over most of it—but I do know that when they first came to this country his mother, in her love for her Jewish prince, dressed him in fancy clothes to go to school and he had to fight his way up the school staircase and down it as the Irish kids teased and tormented the newcomer who could not as yet understand their words. They slashed at his clothes with a knife. He got his own knife and finally they left him alone.

My father went swimming in New York's East River, and once he accepted a dare and swam from a pier in the East Eighties to the far side of the Hell Gate Bridge where the currents were so strong he nearly drowned. I think of him, my brave, valiant, stubborn father alone in the dark water, moving close to the black arc of the railroad bridge, and the whole city, silhouetted behind him, impassive, unwelcoming—I think of him weighed down with feelings and longings and old connections and tender vulnerabilities, potentials for small acts of kindness. He must have cast them all off in the water— ambition alone driving the young arms and legs to the other side of the bridge and back through the dangerous tides again. He told me that during World War I, because his name was Fritz, he was stoned by a group of boys who waited for him in an alley near school. He had been named Fritz in the first place to impress the German gentry of the town where they lived. Now in America, in 1914, that was an unfortunate name to be carrying—it marked him as an enemy, a Kraut. How could the gang of local kids have known he was only a Jewish pretender? After that bloody episode his name was changed. Fred he was called, not so obviously German and certainly not Jewish.

From an Isaac Bashevis Singer story: The blind old man speaks with his crippled friend in a corner of the poorhouse:

> "There is no God."
> "How did the world form?" Motke asked.
> "It grew from itself like a scab."

All Jewish rivers run toward Israel. At first it was believed that God could only be worshiped in the Temple at Jerusalem. Later it was considered that the Messiah would lead the Jews back to Israel where they had been in their beginnings. Zionism is then the yearning for completion—for the righting of

31

a historical injustice—a response to the ever-present insanity of anti-Semitism. Zionism is the logical response to the unavoidable knowledge that Jewishness appears indigestible to other countries. Jews have never been permitted, except for brief moments, to settle comfortably in the Christian or Moslem countries of their adoption. Zionism is also the religious response to the Holocaust. The redemption of the Holy Land and its return to the Jews allows faith to spring like the phoenix from the ruins of Dachau and Auschwitz. But Zionism, religious or political, is still mystical in nature. It requires a passionate emotional commitment to the redemption—it is not a position for rationalists, for universalists. It requires unthinking commitment to one side of the story. It grants the rewards of togetherness. It is not an easy position to adopt late in life without the necessary loyalties and bonds having been forged in childhood, when ideas and ideals and feelings flowed freely and easily in one deep river.

My father had earaches when he was a child. In those days before sulfur and antibiotics, those ear infections could travel to the brain and a child might die. To prevent this the doctors performed a mastoid operation, leaving a hole in the skull that could be covered by hair. After several years in this country my father developed a high fever and a deep throbbing in his ear. The local pharmacist could offer nothing that would stop the pain. My father was taken on the Third Avenue El to the emergency room of Bellevue Hospital—red-brick, horse-drawn ambulances at the door—it resembled then as it does now a dungeon, a place where hope is no more than a form of resistance. In a dramatic race with brain damage the doctors operated on the boy and placed him in a men's charity ward to recover. His father and mother were not allowed to accompany him there. He woke from the operation alone, his head bandaged and in worse pain than before. The man in the bed on one side of him was moaning; his legs had been lost in an industrial accident. The man on the other side called him boy in a kind voice and told him to ring for the nurse if he was thirsty. He talked to the boy about his baby, perhaps dead (my father didn't remember exactly), left behind in Odessa. He spoke for hours in a Yiddish my father claims not to have understood.

In the middle of the hospital night my father woke as a burst of cold air came suddenly over his face. He sat up quickly and saw the nearby window raised to the sash and the man who had talked to him earlier was sitting on the window ledge. The cold wind was blowing against his hospital-issue pajamas. The man turned and saw the boy watching him and without a word jumped. The boy rushed to the window, feeling the strange weight of his newly bandaged head, and saw several stories below blood seeping outward from beneath a body and a piece of bone, standing erect like a bare mast, that had pierced the chest. He saw a strip of torn pajama blow down the street and out of his sight. He was afraid. He went back to bed and closed his eyes. He pretended to be asleep when in a little while the nurses entered the ward. (I have over the years embroidered this story with my own details and imaginings.)

All men who forgot their childhood language, all men who abandoned the synagogue and reached for the brass ring on the American carousel, did not lose their soul in the process, but some of them did. It was a hazard of the times. I know many who like my father wear masks all day and even at night. Here in America the brutality of poverty, the coarseness of life in the tenements, the disrespect for emotions and privacy of the self, were mixed with a new ingredient—hope and pressing expectations for the future. This combination of possibility and deprivation was, in some cases, very bad for the survival of the human spirit.

ANNE ROIPHE

———

The New Jewish Hospital at Hamburg

A hospital for sick and needy Jews
For the poor sons of sorrow thrice accursed
Who groan beneath the heavy, three-fold evil
Of pain and poverty and Judaism.

The most malignant of the three the last is:
That family disease a thousand years old,
The plague they brought with them from the Nile Valley
The unregenerate faith of ancient Egypt.

Incurable deep ill! defying treatment
Of douche and vapor bath and apparatus
Of surgery, and all the healing medicine
This house can offer to its sickly inmates.

Will Time, the eternal goddess in compassion
Root out this dark calamity transmitted
Sire to son? Will one day a descendant
Recover and grow well and wise and happy?

Heinrich Heine

Heine was Germany's most important Jewish poet. His work entered the mainstream of German culture so thoroughly that not even the Nazis could extricate his poems and songs from the culture. Heine was an assimilated Jew from a wealthy business family. He despised his family and remained bitter about their human limitations his life long. But what can we think about this poem about the Jewish hospital at Hamburg?

34

To call Judaism an evil, a dark calamity, and to wish recovery from it—what is this but both self-hate and fashionable Jew hating? Never mind that at least in translation it seems like one dreadful, lumbering piece of poetry. Heine may have (in this poem) confused the emotional pain of his childhood with the condition of his family religion. This is a common enough error and even readers of American writers (Philip Roth, Joseph Heller) may sometimes mix the failure in loving with the flavor of the ethnic and religious experience. These things overlap, but are not quite the same.

Shtetl life had made the Jews more and more strange to their increasingly industrialized and modern neighbors. The rituals, the study of the Talmud, the odd costume, the infusion of all daily routines with the exotic laws of God, the distinctness of speech, the belief in the coming of the Messiah, all these marked Jews off from the emerging modernism of Europe. Worshiping the words of the ancient past, arguing over their exact meaning, repeating rituals precisely because they had been performed that way in antiquity, separated them from their neighbors. The importance they placed on the past, on the honor and rectitude of the old ways and the value of the old words, must have seemed incongruous and even foolish to modern minds impressed with the new hopes of science and machine. People who looked forward to the future as a radical improvement over the past—people who had a concept of progress and human invention—would not be able to spend hours repeating words that their fathers and fathers' fathers had repeated. The Europeans of Heine's era valued change and innovation just the way the pious Jews dreaded it. It was highly possible then to have been a nineteenth-century European Jew and wish for the end of Jewish traditions. Religion itself was in many ways suspect to these new intellectuals of the Enlightenment, and a religion whose historical roots seemed virtually to go back to primitive man naturally would not be admired. Freud refers to the Heine poem, and writing in 1906 believed that science and reason could one day replace the old delusions, the controls of church and the repression of the religious laws. The Jewish religion, the Jewish problem, the unassimilable Jew, these seemed to Freud as to Heine obstacles in the way of the new rationality that they envisioned.

The events of the twentieth century have blasted our hopes for the salvation of mankind through science. Freud's hope for science has proved to be just another illusion. The atomic bomb, the crematoria, did as much to destroy our faith in progress as the false messiah did to destroy the messianic hope of the Jews of the seventeenth century. In the light of the twentieth century, light like a bare bulb in a police station swinging over a suspect's head, we have smaller expectations for the results of human rationalism and unlike Heine we know where the fulminating anti-Semitism of his poem can end.

My brother is an associate professor of hematology at Mount Sinai School of Medicine. He gave me a book called *Genetic Diseases Among Ashkenazi Jews:*

The genetic composition of the Ashkenazi Jews in Israel can be summarized as follows. Ashkenazi Jews are essentially one uniform and homogenous group with respect to all genetic markers in the blood, including blood groups, isozymes, serum proteins and the histocompatibility antigens. When compared to the European populations in which they have lived before migration to Israel, different degrees of closeness in frequencies are demonstrated at different loci however, the overall picture based on all markers is one of distance of the Jews from the European populations, the distribution of Jewish diseases, and among them the Ashkenazi diseases support our contention that *not much* admixture has taken place

36

between the Ashkenazi Jews and their gentile neighbors during the last 700 years or so.

We knew that all along, and yet it is startling to think that a scientist looking through his electronic machines can see the echoes of the origins in the Mediterranean basin of a people who seemed almost more myth than reality. For a while I thought the very idea of a Jewish race a fiction of bigots, a rudeness of racists and borscht-belt comedians. Words like "antigens" and "isozymes" are, however, very convincing, apolitical neutral words. I accept them. It actually is comforting to think of the scientist looking through a powerful lens and finding Sarah, Rebekah, Rachel and the unfortunate, unwanted Leah sending their chemical matter into the future. It comforts and discomforts at the same time. DNA, double helixes, monotheistic, clannish genes, genes programmed on one level for disaster and on another for survival. These genes are identifiable. They didn't need a yellow star.

If the Italians are not called a race then why call the Jews a race? If the Catholics are not called a race then why call the Jews a race? It marks one off to be stigmatized as a racial entity. It gives opportunities to The Violent Ones. But the children of Abraham know that they are more than a collection of religious beliefs. They have not only shared their history they have forged certain genetic clusters. Even if an animal develops camouflage colorations to avoid its predators it retains its basic shape. It is recognizable. "Race" is a word debased by vicious usage. In and of itself it's just a word, like "mountain," "river" or "sky."

———

Asher Ginsberg (Ahad Ha-Am—one of the people) writing in 1893: "It is not imitation as such that leads us to assimilation —the real cause is the original self-effacement which leads us to assimilation through the medium of imitation." Asher Ginsberg thought it was not imitation that was undesirable but self-effacement. A proud, knowledgeable Jewish person could use imitation in his life and enrich his Jewish self without becoming assimilated, or bland, hollow-masked, and so forth. A fine idea but difficult to achieve. Somehow the first steps toward modernism, anthropology, science, universalism, comparative studies of politics and religion, lead to historical perspective, rationalism. These all seem to clash with, not complement Jewishness, at least the Jewishness of the shtetl which depended in part on isolation, the learning of only Jewish themes and history and the absolutism of a community which is convinced of its position as the holy of holies, the chosen among mankind.

Despite the Reform and Reconstructionist movement, the Jewish world tends to dissolve in assimilationist waters as the absolute isolating factors of the religion are diminished. From the beginnings of history the people with the strongest armies, the powers of governmental control, taxation and punishment have spread their own culture into the dominated areas. Might tends to make religion and culture, whatever its moral worth.

The Syrians, the Babylonians, the Egyptians, the Romans, the Greeks, the Turks, and, as we have seen in the nineteenth-century workings of imperialism, the French and the Germans, and even the Americans make their ways seem desirable just by economic and political control. The spread of the dominant group's religion, the assimilation of one local group into another follows behind (in some cause-linked way), associated with the success of armies. From its very beginnings Jewish history contains a fight against assimilation or imitation.

"Thou shalt have no other God before me. Thou shalt have no graven images," were the commandments given to combat just such temptations. In the desert of Moses there were assimilationists who strove to build idols and borrow habits from native populations. Moses himself despaired of keeping his people on their path even at its more simple stages of development. The Old Testament is filled with examples of people who strayed from the truth or the true way. The prophets are always promising God's retribution for just this sin of adapting to the strangers' ways and sliding into the strangers' style. The prophets, with more thunderous prose but no less determination than the suburban rabbis, kept hammering at the evils of leaving the Jewish way. In a sense they created the form followed by the rabbis of Great Neck and Brentwood today. This seesawing tension between those who stay with the religion of their fathers and those who stray away is an old story, old but not worn out.

The nature of the fight has not changed. The rabbi must make it very clear that the greatest sin is to betray the group by marrying the outsider or imitating the outsider's customs or forms of worship. It is amazing that the Jews have held out so long in alien territory and they have not succumbed to the blandishments of Canaanite gods, of Babylonian gods, of Greek gods, of Roman gods and of course the powerful Bloody God of Mercy himself, Jesus Christ. The holdout is one of history's paradoxes, exceptions that prove the rule.

It is of course quite conceivable that without the helpful benefits of the continual persecution of the Jewish communities the ancient war against assimilation would have been lost long ago.

A double force has preserved Jewry. The isolating marks of Jewish life—the intense saturation of Jewish persons in their tradition, their learned pride in their differences and their way, their tendency to segregate themselves from the influences of the outside world—these have worked to preserve the nation, together with the brutality and viciousness of the peoples of the non-Jewish world, be they Egyptians and their pharaohs or Spaniards encouraged by Catholic bishops or czars with unruly soldiers. The non-Jewish world seems to produce antibodies that attack the Jewish foreign matter—again and again host bodies have rejected the Jewish people they first welcomed into their midst. Persecution, a history of persecution, contributes to Jewish cohesion, and Jewish nationhood suffers some attrition when assimilation becomes or appears to become possible. How much, how far, will it go? The American experience may provide the answer.

Another way to look at it, like the ocean tide always rising and ebbing, particles of the Jewish peoples are always pulled away in the strong currents of social forces, and at the same time other parts of the Jewish community are remaining fixed, rigid, unchanging, inwardly turned, preservative of the past and its traditions; together, those pulling away and those pulling back, both constitute the whole of the Jewish experience, just as the ocean is the ocean whether the tide is in or out; whatever the movements of the water the combined totality of the tides constitutes the sea with its great variety within and its constancy.

Rabbi Israel Shapiro of the city of Grodzisk in Poland told his Jews as they assembled on the railroad station platform at Treblinka that "these are the last real birth pangs of the Messiah. You are all blessed to have merited the honor of being sacrifices and your ashes will serve to purify all Israel." To die for a cause is far better than to die without purpose or meaning and the psychological need for the rabbi to make that speech is of course understandable and should be respected. But I am angry with Rabbi Shapiro. The poor pitiable fool! If there is any need to be purified it lies in God, without Whose permission and cooperation the Holocaust could not have come to be. It is God's purity that is in doubt, not that of the Jewish nation.

There were apparently some Jews in Łódź who just before their forced departure for the camps spent the day fasting, reading Psalms, and then they opened the Ark and convoked a solemn din Torah (a religious ritual in which man accuses God of wrongdoing), and forbade God to punish His people further. It's hard not to ridicule such pious men, but how can one not be moved by the extreme to which they had been taken? Taught throughout their lives to beg, plead, entreat God, they tried in this terrible circumstance to order God to return to some kind of moral position, to cease His wanton destruction. God, of course, was silent. Commanding God had no better results than begging Him, which in turn was no better than ignoring Him.

Rabbi Daniel of Kelme in Lithuania asked permission of the SS captain to address his people one last time as they stood in the freshly dug trenches on the outskirts of town—two thousand of them, men, women, old people and babies. The request was granted. The rabbi spoke. He told his people of the honor and the dignity in dying for God—of performing the traditional Kiddush Hashem (the santification of the death of martyrs, those who would not convert or abandon the faith of their fathers). The Einsatzgruppen then proceeded to slaughter the entire gathering, including the eloquent rabbi. To the pious man, the Kiddush Hashem is a sensible and sense-giving act, bravely insisting on order in the midst of apparent chaos. To the humanist, however, the Kiddush Hashem is an obscenity—a God who would permit it is dishonored in the act. It is difficult to pay respect to the God of the Holocaust. It is possible to hate Him. Hate, of course, will, like love, change nothing. It only weighs one down with a festering, aching, painful soul-state that threatens to consume the personality and warp the mind. It is far better to become an atheist or at least an agnostic and repress the hatred—not forgive—never forgive, but turn away, sidestep, search for other explanations of human existence. I tend toward explanations that involve chemistry, protoplasm, big bangs, supernovas, universes that began without moral implications, promises or mutual arrangements between man and God.

My father told me how his father had taken his family to the Third Avenue El as soon as they had arrived from Ellis Island. They were looking for a cousin who was prepared to house the new immigrants. As they rode the train they looked in the windows of the sweatshops. They looked down on the push-carts and the hanging washes. The noise of the unfamiliar El overwhelmed them, along with the shouts and cries of the people in the streets. My grandfather had a change of heart. He took his family back to the offices of the shipping company. He wanted to book passage for them all to return to Europe. As the children huddled around their bags in the waiting room, my grandfather counted out his money at the ticket window. He did not have enough. There was no choice but to remain in America. Once again they mounted the steps of the El, headed uptown.

Several days later my grandfather went apartment hunting. He walked all over Manhattan till he came to Fifth Avenue. This he found quite to his liking. He asked the price of an apartment in the English he had been studying on the boat. The doorman told him. My grandfather was delighted, only two hundred dollars. He brought back his family with their bags and their expectations raised high. America, he had told them, was truly a paradise. The doorman and the elevator man and the manager all came out and laughed at the shabby family gathered in the elegant lobby. It was two hundred dollars a month, not two hundred dollars a year.

Asher Ginsberg writes in 1904: "Our very Hebrew language has no present tense, only a past and a future. The past be-

comes a mirror of the future. We never live in the present."
The Zionist writer means only that in 1904 Hebrew was the
language of the ancient home and the promised land of the
future. For the moment it was the tool of the scholar and the
method of the pious but not a living secular tongue. Asher
Ginsberg may also have been thinking about the historicity
that forms most of Judaic thought and practice: that is, we
do things this way because it was said or done that way before, we repeat the actions, words and gestures of old sages
long since turned to dust. This constantly walking forward
with the mind firmly focused on the past or on a utopian future exposes the Jews to dangers. Martin Luther thought that
because we missed the arrival of the true Messiah we are no
longer God's Chosen People. We lost our status as the favorite child and didn't notice. Even if that strikes the Jewish ear
as arrogant and unnecessary, it is true that all that thinking
about the past provides opportunities for others to attack and
destroy in the present. The distinction between man and beast
lies in the human gift to remember the past and anticipate the
future. But the animal who lives only in the present also knows
how to survive and it seems possible that there are limits to
man's superiority over the beast; in fact, good instincts, healthy
drives, quick responses in the present, are animal qualities that
are perhaps more worthy of our attention than some theological schemes for future redemption. Our fate may depend on
our remembering our humble connections with four-legged
furry ones, mammals, marsupials, amphibians. A language
that has no present life may be too rarefied—it can become an
equivalent of gazing at the moon in rhapsody while walking
along a narrow road, along angular cliffs.

In Israel the Hebrew language has a reality in the present.
The Jewish manner of ranking past, present and future may
change now and the imbalances be redressed. In Israel the
Hebrew language may mutate the way languages naturally do
and the verb "to be," which now does not exist in the Hebrew
present tense, will find its own form. "To be" is a verb that

should have a present. This is one reason why Israel is so important to Jews everywhere.

———

The French philosopher, E. M. Cioran, who was born in Rumania and educated in the Greek Orthodox Church, writes romantically, a little hysterically, about the Jews:

"To be a man is a drama; to be a Jew is another. Hence the Jew has the privilege of living our condition twice over. No creatures less anonymous. Without them who could breathe in our cities? They maintain a state of fever, without which any agglomeration becomes a province, a dead city is a city without Jews. Effective as a ferment and a virus, they inspire a double sense of fascination and discomfort. Our reaction to them is almost always murky. Do not accuse them of being parvenus: How could they be, when they have passed through and left their mark on so many civilizations? If they possess a wisdom, it is the wisdom of exile, the kind which teaches how to triumph over a unanimous sabotage, how to believe oneself chosen when one has lost everything: the wisdom of defiance. And yet they are called cowards! It is true that they can cite no spectacular victory: but their very existence, is that not one? . . . Whatever they do and wherever they go, their mission is to keep watch, this is the command of their immemorial status as aliens. . . . Their penchant for utopias is merely a memory projected into the future, a vestige converted into an ideal. But it is their fate, even as they aspire to paradise to collide with the Wailing Wall" (E. M. Cioran, *The Temptation to Exist*, trans. Richard Howard [New York: Times Books, 1972]).

All this is very elegant. It is rather complimentary and even inspiring, but somehow I'm suspicious. Too much praise, too many inflated and high-blown words, seem like the opposite coin of virulent anti-Semitism. So much awe is a cover, a face that must have another expression. Besides, when one thinks of a little Jewish child playing with paper dolls in a window seat in Prague as the Nazis fly over the bridges at the outskirts of town, or a Jewish grandmother wrapping up the remains of lunch to take with her on the train to the camps, all the words disappear and in the extremity only human beings remain. I am afraid of the rhetoric on both sides. Rhetoric, even if elegant, appears to have the quality of a magic chant that releases the genie of evil.

The Memoirs of Gluckel of Hameln, translated by Marvin Lowenthal (New York: Schocken Books, 1977):

Gluckel of Hameln began her memoirs in 1690 when she was forty-four years old. She was a widow with twelve living children, eight of them still unmarried and living at home. She describes in seven small chapters the family history, her business affairs, the deaths of four of her children and the bankruptcy and disgrace of her second husband. A pious Jewish woman, she weaves quotes from the Scriptures into her tales and exhorts her children to set aside time each day for prayer and study. When sickness and death enter the house, she believes that God is punishing her for imperfections of character. Her theology is, of course, ordinary and of no special distinction, but as she writes we see how religion sinks like milk into a slice of bread, saturating her life, her business, her dealings with her children, relatives and all the banalities of daily obligations. Her business head is of the best and her devoted husband Chayim Hameln depended on her alone and after his death she went to the fairs selling goods and jewelry, giving and getting credit for large amounts of money. She reports in great detail all the negotiations around the marriages of her children. The dowry settlements seemed to be a major business activity. She records for the future the amounts of each of the dowries and the social importance of the various wedding parties she attended. This matter of making a marriage could take months, and in order to make the best matches for her children she journeyed to the Jewish communities as far away as Amsterdam, Vienna and Berlin. She travels while kings are at war.

Gluckel also reports running from the plague in Hamburg and she sadly describes keeping her father-in-law's trunks while he, having sold all his earthly goods, waits for the false messiah, Sabbatai Zevi, to call the Jews to Zion.

Gluckel believes this messiah was false because the Jews are not yet ready for redemption—but the next Messiah she still believes will mark the end of human suffering.

Gluckel is the archetypal Jewish wife, mother and businessperson. She writes: "Every two years I had a baby, I was so tormented with worries as is everyone in a house full of children. God be with them, and I thought myself more heavily burdened than anyone else in the whole world and that no one suffered so much from their children as I. Little I knew, poor fool, how fortunate I was when I seated my children 'like olive plants round my table.' "

There are many interesting things to be said about Gluckel. The first must be to question what caused her to write at all. She was alone and among the very first. She claims that she is telling her children the history of their family so that they will know where they come from and who their people were. But I expect that's only an excuse, a rational face on the less explicable impulse to let one's life stand as an example, to give it some sense and some order, to take some perspective and make peace with the chaos within; a writer's impulse that does not change with the passage of centuries or the degree of sophistication. Gluckel was not, by our standards, a very imaginative woman—the confines of her world were rigid and inhibiting. She was, after all, only a woman, forbidden scholarship and the exercise of intellect. She was a person of the ghetto, for whom the Christian world with its art and sculpture—its blooming Renaissance—could not be reinvented within the provincial confines of Jewish Hamburg and her merchant class that hung so precariously onto the edges of the greater society. And yet she wanted to write down what she saw and what she knew . . . it was Defoe's impulse and Erica Jong's. It was with a writer's eye that she reports the gory details of her husband's death and it was with a writer's impulse that she records the last description in the book.

In the synagogue at Metz a terrible, rumbling, thundering noise was heard on the roof and the women, who were all gathered upstairs, panicked, thinking the building was falling down on them. They pushed and clawed their way to the single staircase. They trampled over each other and six of them were crushed to death. The roof, it turned out, was not crumbling and no one ever found out what had caused the strange and fatal noise. Gluckel thought perhaps the females in the congregation were being punished by God for a fight that had broken out in their galleries a few weeks earlier. The event as told by Gluckel has some glimmer of understanding of the divine ironies and that is certainly the beginning of literature. Gluckel writes for the same reason all writers take up the task, with a secret agenda: to complain, to protest the way things are, to attempt to understand, and if that isn't possible, at the least to leave evidence of what happened, evidence that might permit someone in the future to understand what those in the present cannot; and if the future has no better grasp of events at the very least it can register the complaint.

Gluckel was among the first writers in the Western world to notice that babies and dowries, relations of in-laws and the rise and fall of individual bank accounts were in fact subjects for the written page—subjects for the next generation to wonder over. Her act of writing, an act so isolated, in a Jewish world where men had the power of the word and used it only to explicate and weave about the Torah and matters of mighty philosophy, her act of writing is an act so daring, a compulsion so pure, that one can only marvel.

Gluckel reports on the dangers that surrounded the Hof-juden (those Jews who served as advisers to the city-state governors or petty princes of the time). She reports on their good fortune in times of favor and of their going to prison and being executed when the winds of state changed. She talks of the difficulties of a Jew who might die attending a fair in Leipzig and forfeit all his property rights as well as a decent burial (Jews were not permitted cemeteries in Leipzig and not allowed legal ownership or inheritance rights). She reports on the murders of several Jewish merchants and the fears of the Jewish community that in their search for justice they might antagonize the Gentiles. Her attitude toward anti-Semitism is interesting: Without anger or surprise, she appears to accept the random cruelties in the unpredictable Christian world of the seventeenth century the way we might interpret the damages of tropical storms, typhoons or earthquakes.

Since Gluckel believes in the coming of the Messiah she also carries the Jewish guilt for Jewish wickedness that has kept him waiting in the clouds for a more morally perfect day to make his entrance.

Gluckel, although an independent and shrewd business-woman, is certainly no early feminist—how, after all, could she be? As her husband lay dying in great pain she says, "Dearest heart, shall I embrace you, I am unclean?"

He answers, "God forbid, my child, it will not be long before you take your cleansing."

It was by then, Gluckel tells us, too late. Gluckel could not openly rebel but she reports this incident with perhaps a touch of bitterness—or is the bitterness of a twentieth-century view? Marriages were arranged and took place at a very young age, eleven or twelve. The sexual development of both men and women had to be affected by the strict regulations around menstruation and the sense of the woman as being unclean or too seductive. The wearing of the wig and the placing of the woman outside the pale of the serious religious practices (the laws of divorce, property, adultery) made her her husband's inferior.

Nowhere does Gluckel report a sexual feeling. She feels free to talk on endlessly about money and only about sex does she become reticent. She takes a new husband after eleven years of widowhood because she mistakenly thinks it financially advisable. She does not speak of needing male attentions in any other way. Her sensibility is the reverse of the modern, where women will talk on about orgasm and love and never about bank accounts and bond issues. We seem to have shifted bad taste from one area to another.

Gluckel is a strong matriarch. She seems, at least from her telling of it, like the very stuff that Jewish dreams are made of, what Mrs. Portnoy would have wanted for her Alex, what every rabbi tells the bride under the chuppa (wedding canopy) she must be. Gluckel's strength appears to come from her piety—but of course her religiosity could simply be the mantle in which her strength goes about—the coverings of her naturally gutsy soul. "Trust in God," she says over and over again. She knows what is right and what is not and she never needs Valium or a therapist or even an investment counselor. She is committed to behaving morally in all business dealings and nearly goes bankrupt on several occasions bailing out a swindler son whose sense of honor is less certain than hers. She lives securely within a network of family relationships, brothers-in-law, sisters, children and their in-laws. The loyalty of the group to one another, in helping to arrange marriages, in money matters, in providing protection and support, is apparent on every page. Gluckel would not understand our complaints of isolation, loneliness; not only would she not know the word "narcissism," but one would never be able to explain it to her. Without the conception of romantic love she was not tortured by its absence and in fact seems to have loved her first husband as well as most. The second she might have

49

loved, but he met with financial disaster, and money and love were bound together in that place in a way we can only struggle to understand.

One of her descendants was Heinrich Heine, who would probably have found her dull company. She had none of the choices open to the young women of his circle. She had none of the choices we have today. She had no opportunity to become an airline attendant, a professor of Greek history or a vice-president of a bank. She couldn't eat the food of all nations and she'd never seen the ballet, the opera or a movie. Her able mind was dwarfed by its place in history and yet when reading her book I am aware of her comforts. Writing on the loss of her husband, Gluckel says:

"We, my children, have no friend on whom we may depend save God, who will ever stand by you. You have lost your true and good father, but your heavenly father abideth forever and He will not desert you as long as you serve Him in faithfulness . . . and if, God forbid, you suffer punishment, you will have naught to blame but yourself and your own deeds."

Her world made sense. It had clean moral edges, and while the guilt she takes on herself and gives to others seems enormous and capable of ending up in a Woody Allen movie with egg all over its face, she does not for a second endure the random emptiness of the absurdist universe known all too well by us. On balance her condition seems enviable.

Gluckel was forty-four when she began to write. I am forty-four as I begin this book. Gluckel would consider the similar numbers a sign from God. I consider it an odd coincidence.

My youngest daughter Becky had entered kindergarten. Sometime in October they have a parents' meeting. My husband and I have been through this many times before. We are casual, relaxed, maybe a little bored, but contented nevertheless. We lean close into each other as we cross the threshold. We are aware of marking a passage for our last child. Immediately we feel the excitement of the new parents, the young ones whose first child is now meeting the larger world. They are testing their parenthood in a new school arena. This is their public debut as the "daddy" and the "mommy." They are excessively proud and in no small degree anxious—their need to be liked and to have their child admired fills the room with a sweet tension. They are dressed for the occasion in what appear to be new clothes, so shining is this moment. The teacher explains the daily routine. We discuss reading readiness and math games. One mother asks about nutrition because her daughter is a vegetarian, and a father wants to know when his daughter can begin to work in computer programming. We meet the music teacher and the special science teacher who tells us about the rabbits and the guinea pigs. Juice and cookies are served. Unsteadily, we stand up from the little tables around which we have gathered, Gullivers all in a Lilliputian world. It is time to talk with the other parents.

A young woman finds out my husband is a psychoanalyst.

"Come and see my child's picture." She pulls us along. "There," she says, "look, isn't it wonderful? She has such a strong sense of identity, don't you think so, Doctor?"

My husband smiles and nods and makes admiring noises.

"Look at that Jewish star, look at the picture of her family." There on the white page is a large Star of David, all colored in bright yellow, and under it a group of stick figures, all smiling—the family: mother, father, brother, self and baby sister. "She knows she's Jewish," says the mother, with a sweet and tender smile. "Jewish and family; those are the two pillars of her identity. Isn't that really healthy?" says the mother almost bouncing up and down in pleasure. I slid away as my husband makes more admiring noises.

I drift over to the other side of the room and look at my own child's painting. Its green and blue smudges running together and some paint drips along the edges trace the motion of the brush. This is the sort of painting that not even the most philistine of Philistines would suggest could hang in New York's Museum of Modern Art. My child has no Jewish identity. She has no non-Jewish identity. She hasn't yet heard the word. She has no particular place that she knows of in the social order. She doesn't yet know there is a social order. She still divides the world into animals and people. I look carefully at her blue and green smudges. Is it unhealthy? How, then, can I give her an identity, a place? I feel a deep sadness, as if I suddenly noticed my child had a chronic illness and as if I were to blame for that illness.

"Hannah knows the Hebrew alphabet," says the young mother, still talking with my husband. I recover my balance. My child's psychosocial identity will have to do without symbols and foreign tongues. She will have to build it slowly. She will have to make choices herself later. She will be different from Hannah but not necessarily worse. I look around the room. None of the Christian children have drawn crosses or churches. I see many more blobs and I begin to feel better.

The following month my daughter comes home from school and reports, "Hannah is Jewish," she says. "Her daddy came to school and made us potato pancakes and told us all about Channukah."

"You're Jewish too," I say. "It's just that we don't go to temple and celebrate the holidays."

"Why not?" says my child.

I try to explain what a humanist is. I realize I have never used the word before in conversation. It sounds artificial, unreal, pompous. I am unconvinced. I hear myself stumbling. "When you're older you'll understand," I hedge.

She runs off. I've bought some time. I congratulate myself . . . at least I had the good judgment not to try to explain existentialism—but why did I tell her she was Jewish? In doing so I identified Jewishness as something other than a religion and I firmly bound her on Abraham's altar (she will not forget that I said we were Jewish).

Hannah's father is an Israeli engineer. All Israelis are, of course, more Jewish than anyone else. Maybe one day there will be no Jews in the galut—the ones like me will have assimilated out of existence and the others will have taken their credit cards and moved to Israel. It is true, as Emil Fackenheim said in the *Encyclopedia Judaica*, yearbook, 1978: "The heart of every authentic response to the Holocaust, religious and secularist, Jewish and non-Jewish is a commitment to the state of Israel." Israel is the new solution to the Jewish problem. If we have a homeland like any other nation we will be protected, we will be less vulnerable to the new waves of anti-Semitism, which the future is bound to create. The safety of Israel is of intense mythic and realistic proportions to all American Jews. The drama of the Palestine Liberation Organization (PLO) and the Israeli people has become a kind of morality play, a combat of dragon and knight that promises to shed light on God's position and the whole human enigma. Of course who plays dragon and who plays knight is in the eye of the audience, and since this is a modern drama there is no claim made for objective reality—we swim in our own truths.

I read in the morning's *New York Times* a eulogy for a young Israeli killed by terrorists in an attack on a tourist bus. The writer describes the young boy's grandfather who wrote poetry and grew peach trees in the arid land. The writer describes the young boy who played the flute in a family of musicians and talked about his interest in languages and art. One reads and despairs at the loss of this so promising life, so cultured, so Jewish, so rich in potential for thought and kindness. A few pages back in the same newspaper is a photograph of an Arab mother holding in her arms the dead body of her boy. He also seems to be about twelve years old. He had been killed in an Israeli retaliative bombing of border villages that might have harbored members of the PLO. The boy's body is covered with dust from the fallen plaster of the modest home and his mother has no shoes on her feet. One suspects that this boy did not play the flute and his grandfather might not have known a sonnet from a ballad, but the pity falls with equal weight on both sets of frail shoulders and the pain of loss is the same whatever the degree of education of the parents. The mark of Cain is shared.

Wanting with all one's soul for Israel to survive within secure borders, one can still recognize the dead as dead and belonging to all humanity; that is humanism (if only I could find a way to explain it to the children). There seems to be a continuing dialectic between the universalist and particular response—redemption has always been understood as one group's victory over another. It has always been bought at someone else's expense. In freeing the Jews from bondage in the house of the pharaohs, God sent plagues on the heads of the Egyptian children. He killed off firstborn sons, and if that didn't cause enough grief to Egyptian parents, He drowned an entire army in the Red Sea. The group view, while uniting those within, always turns the enemy into a faceless, disposable mass. At every known moment of recorded history someone has been made to play the role of gook.

Jews have always included the broader human condition in their ritual and thought. On Passover the drops of water may be taken from a glass to symbolize God's tears for His children —the Egyptian soldiers who drowned in the Red Sea. Jews identify with boat people everywhere. Since the first days of Jewish Emancipation in the nineteenth century, Jews have been in the vanguard of all idealistic political surges. It was two Jewish boys who were killed in the swamps of the South as the civil rights movement began. Jewishness is the soil of humanism but it is also true that any fierce loyalty to one group makes possible distortions or subtle reductions in the perceived values or rights of the outsider.

A fear of tribalism is part of being humanist. Another authentic response to the Holocaust is to resist all efforts to separate human beings into categories of greater or lesser value —to use culture, or skin color, or blood type to select one life over another is to dishonor those who died in the ovens and the trains and the ditches—the victims of SS and Einsatzgruppen—the victims of nationalism (tribalism) gone amok.

———————

Of course the State of Israel means more than the political protection of Jews persecuted in the past and the future. It means more than a refuge from catastrophe—although that in itself might be validation enough. The State of Israel signifies redemption, the fulfillment of God's covenant to Abraham. It offers a religious confirmation of the worth and the truth of the long line of struggle from past to present. The Israeli chief rabbi opens all official occasions with the prayer: "Father in Heaven, Rock of Israel and her Redeemer, bless the State of Israel, the beginnings of the dawn of our redemption." (There are plenty of secular Israelis, the majority of the population, who must listen to this prayer like one listens to the rain on the rooftops, a familiar sound, within which one may feel cozy or bored depending on the moment's mood.)

It is easy enough to see that future generations may cele- brate and commemorate the events of the founding of Israel and the Holocaust in combined or associated ceremonies. The Passover, the joy of Purim, the mourning of Tisha B'ab, these may be joined with the higher and even holier holidays of the twentieth century.

Rabbi Irving Greenberg, former chairman of the Depart- ment of Jewish Studies at City College and head of the Na- tional Jewish Resource Center, says, "Faith in the God of History demands that an unprecedented act of destruction be matched by an unprecedented act of redemption and this has happened." Rabbi Greenberg, the husband of Blu Greenberg,

brilliantly spins out arguments reconciling Jews to the cataclysmic events of recent history. Rabbi Greenberg even accepts
that some Jews will have to reject God and doubt His existence. He even believes that secular Jews in Israel are part of the
redemption and therefore part of the religious experience of
the Jewish nation. Rabbi Greenberg believes there must be a
new covenant between man and God after the Holocaust and
he wants that new covenant to include women and to use as its
symbol something other than circumcision, which, after all,
marks only the male.

I am an admirer of Rabbi Greenberg. If I could be converted to a religious view, Rabbi Greenberg could do it because
he does not dismiss the depth of my religious anxiety and
he respects the legitimacy of anger toward the God of his
fathers and mine too, I suppose. Today, in the early stages
of writing this book, I turn my mind to stone, I close the doors,
I don't want to allow Rabbi Greenberg to convince me of the
inconceivable, because if the Temple has been twice destroyed
and if every little band of crusaders can claim a synagogue or
two of victims and if the Inquisition and the cossacks and
the Turks all had their piece of Jewish flesh, why then should
I believe in the Chosen People? This idea that Israel is the redemption may be only another tantalizing illusion—a kind of
twentieth-century Sabbatai Zevi. It may be the prelude to a
more total disaster, probably this time destroying all mankind.

In the case of a thermonuclear Armageddon, the Jews would
have served, as Rabbi Greenberg points out, as those canaries
or parrakeets taken by miners into the deepest caves. The
little birds die instantly when small amounts of gas begin to
leak through the tunnels. They function as an alarm system.
So the Holocaust may have been a warning that mankind is
down too far. If the Gulag and Auschwitz were in fact theological warning devices, the survival of the species is not very likely.

Rabbi Greenberg looks like a scholarly basketball player—a
long thin line of mental activity. He talks with incredible
speed as if his thoughts are rattling against his lips, pushing

to get out. He speaks quietly and his hands move gently in odd nervous rhythms. His children call him Abba (Hebrew for father). They know that he believes that each child is an act of resistance against Hitler, that each of the five lives he has helped create is a force of affirmation, of particular Jewish affirmation. Rabbi Greenberg speaks of a temporary silence, an interruption in the dialogue between man and God. He rejects the idea of justifying the Holocaust in any way that would appear obscene or ridiculous to the millions burned in the ovens. He rejects, then, Gluckel's position that pain comes because of personal sins. He says one cannot accuse the children thrown into burning fires. Jewish guilt and responsibility for what has happened to them are concepts of a simpler age, a pretechnological time when events seemed more under the control of individual choice and less the result of the incomprehensible forces of darkness and night. Rabbi Greenberg speaks of moments of doubt and moments of faith as alternating with each other—as possible within the same person. He considers maintaining contradictory positions as a reasonable way to live. Rabbi Greenberg thinks a new religious position can be achieved by allowing the dialectic of doubt and faith to rage as it will. He feels we can no longer speak to God with the same respect and in the forms of the past. He anticipates new rituals and new symbolic forms to shape religious life.

Blu Greenberg is an attractive, vital, solid woman. She has authority and strength, a natural aura of command that makes her a leader among women. She has a certainty about her that has banished whimsy or doubt. She is direct, blunt and honest. She has also a quality of reserve, of a profound shyness that adds complexity. If her husband, Rabbi Irving Greenberg, is a dreamer, a visionary, a poet, a philosopher, she is of the earth, dependable, a person to be near in times of emergency or crisis. Blu thinks that the Messiah will come—if not in her lifetime then in her children's or grandchildren's lifetime. All of her life (her father is also an Orthodox rabbi), without holding her breath, she has believed in His coming. She had no doubt at all. I do not understand. How can she believe in the Messiah, after all that has happened! Blu looks at me puzzled. "How can you not believe in His coming after all that has happened? The world could use redeeming."

Palestine was originally taken by force from the native inhabitants. Joshua, David, Saul were at war with Philistines, Amorites, Canaanites, Moabites and other idol worshipers for centuries. I wonder if Arafat and David could understand each other. The old tradition of might and power of the superior army justifies removing Arab families from their old lands and equally justifies Arab attempts to regain that land. Titus, Cyrus, Trajan were only the earliest foreign interests playing off the natives to gain dominion for themselves. What are empires (from Cyrus to the Third Reich) but tribes suffering from terminal gigantism—making ancient tribal claims—particularly the tribal right to take away by force other peoples' land and reduce them to slaves?

Rabbi Jochanan said, "When you see an age in which suffering pours like a stream then hope for Him." John Calvin insisted that the righteous judgment of God had struck the Jews with blindness because they rejected the light of heaven. Both of these are admirable examples of pretzel-thought, amazing! Freud says early cultures told stories of the god—the father—struggling with his son, and in those stories the son always eventually wins and overthrows the father. The religion of the son (the Christian religion) has, in fact, replaced the religion of the father (Jewish). Christianity, as it became accepted throughout the Western world, then committed an anthropological form of deicide against the religion of Jehovah (God). This is indeed a kind of cultural repetition of the Cronos myth. If we ever had a mother religion, would there be an end to anti-Semitism, a reconciliation of father and son?

Freud has described the origins of religious thought in the child's helplessness, and in man's need to control his sexual and aggressive instincts in order to create a viable social unit for the preservation of the group. The sense of helplessness and the need for control contribute to the creation of the illusions of religion. He says: "When the child grows up and finds that he is destined to remain a child forever, and that he can never do without protection against unknown and mighty powers, he invests them with the traits of the father figure; he creates for himself the gods, of whom he is afraid, whom he seeks to propitiate and to whom he nevertheless entrusts the task of protecting him. Thus the longing for the father explanation is identical with the other, the need for protection against the consequences of human weakness. The child's defensive reaction to his helplessness gives the characteristic features to the adult's reaction to his own sense of helplessness, i.e., the formation of religion."

Psychoanalyst Dr. Martin Bergmann has invited my husband and me to join a meeting of a group of psychoanalysts who gather every third Friday during the winter months to discuss the particular emotional and developmental problems of the Holocaust survivors and their children. They are slowly preparing a book. We meet in the Central Park West apartment of a Dr. and Dr. Gruen. Instantly I am at home in the apart-

ment; all over New York, transplanted European-Jewish analysts have recreated the style of their hastily abandoned homes.
The furniture is heavy mahogany, the drawings on the walls
are of Venice, or Palermo, or ancient Athens. Pots and pots of
green plants sit on the dark wines of Persian carpets; they lean
toward the graying lace of the draperies. The colors of everything are soft browns and yellows. There are books everywhere
and of course the requisite portrait of Freud.

It is a form of interior decorating that evokes Europe in the
1930s. These apartments are faintly sad—an out-of-placeness, a
memory of violence and abruptness, hangs about the good
china and the bookcases—and yet I am always comforted in
these homes; intelligence, dignity, a certain propriety have survived. I feel a little brash, raw, uneducated, a frontierperson on
a trip back to Boston. I feel the newness of my culture.

Most of the other doctors at the meeting are also refugees,
from Prague, from Berlin, from Budapest. My husband, born
in Brooklyn, is among the minority. In each of the 110 cases
this group has studied so far, the survivors' children have
shown severe developmental difficulties that directly repeat or
recapitulate the traumatic events that scarred their parents'
lives. This evening the group discusses a case presented by my
husband of a mother of a baby observed in a normal nursery
as part of a normal development project on child care in the
Bronx borough of New York. This mother, B., was six years
old at the end of the war when, with her mother and sisters,
she came out of hiding and eventually escaped across the
Czech border. B.'s father had been shot in the streets while
foraging for food for his family when B. was only two years
old. After that they moved many times and for at least three
years she was separated from her mother and hidden in the
country.

Now she was bringing up her own baby and had married an
American businessman. After having apparently recovered
from an acute postpartum depression, this mother left her
baby every month or so to go traveling with her husband. It

was clear to the pediatrician and all the observers at the clinic that the baby was suffering acutely from these many separations and was having major trouble sleeping. This mother put the baby to sleep in an unusual manner, without giving the baby the comfort of either a bottle or a special blanket. The baby was patted on the back by the mother until she fell asleep. An interview with the grandmother disclosed that while the family was in hiding she had always put her own daughter (the baby's mother) to sleep exactly that way to avoid any cries from the child, which of course could have been dangerous to the whole family.

The doctors talked on for two hours about this baby who barely smiled and developed odd biting and hair-pulling behavior. They talked about the trauma of the mother who was separated so often from her own mother and was now repeating the unfortunate events on the child of the new country, on the child of another time. The doctors talked on about disturbance of object relations, the effect of childhood depression, on the odd depressed quality of the child so like the mother's. They reported the many times they had witnessed a mother's compulsion to reproduce the neglect experienced in her own childhood on the next generation. They conjectured as to whether B. had actually seen her father shot. They talked about the constipation the baby developed and the connection of bowel control with fear of loss of parents. They talked about the baby's reduced verbal ability in light of the long silences that the mother, as a child, had experienced out of necessity. They talked about bottle feeding, toilet training and survivor guilt. They mentioned that for survivors there seems to be a heightened sense of life and death about matters that others are able to handle more casually. In the survivors they have studied, high levels of anxiety seem never to totally subside, and around life's trivial obstacles they reemerge. As the doctors talked on I felt a kind of glorious exhilaration, a grand love for all of them (not just leftover transference feelings from my own past analysis); I felt triumphant. The Nazi establishment had thought the life of a Jewish baby was not worth the half-cent of gas it would cost to kill that baby in the crematorium. When gas became costly and ran short they threw the infants and children directly into burning ovens. The Jewish baby was not only without human value, it was an enemy creature that must be destroyed as cheaply as possible.

Here in 1980, in New York, these doctors were discussing in infinite detail every aspect of a single Jewish baby's life, its sleep habits, its bottle feeding, its vocabulary, its mood, its aggressive instincts, its libido organization. The victory was total. The baby was again a human being; its psychology, its brief life experiences, consisting of the most primitive, earliest interweaving of biological and psychological needs, were subject to these grown people's concern and attention, their intellectual and compassionate interest. The psychoanalysts' victory over the Nazis was to reassert once again the absolute complexity of life and the value of even a mind so small and insignificant as this infant's. In an environment where peekaboo games and bowel movements are given thought, then once again all human life is sanctified. The meeting itself was an ethical communion.

———

"Why are you so concerned about the Holocaust?" asks my twenty-one-year-old stepdaughter. "I thought you were writing a book on assimilation."

During one of her recesses from medical school, we are having lunch with her male friend who is a graduate student in English. His mother is a born-again Christian. He himself once believed in Zen but now is leaning toward Freud. He says that Christian theology makes it easier to accept the Holocaust because of its emphasis on the Apocalypse, or the world to come. Christianity, he points out, has its tradition of martyrs and it makes a great fuss about life after death and contends that this world's existence is of no matter.

"The martyrs had a choice," I explain. "They were not a people exterminated."

My stepdaughter's friend looks at me surprised. Why am I so vehement? Why is my hand holding my wine glass shaking? I tell them about an Episcopal minister who was the president of an Eastern college for many years. I had asked him how he reconciled the idea of a Christian God with the events of the Holocaust. He saw no difficulty: "Evil is evil," he said. "It's always been the same. If young Oxford or Cambridge boys are sent to die in the Crimea or the Rhine, if people kill people, it's evil and God has permitted the evil in the world so that human beings can struggle to perfect themselves, to improve their characters. Evil is an obstacle. Suffering is part of growth toward God, and the Holocaust is just another event in history where evil temporarily holds forth."

Of course, I ramble on, the Holocaust isn't the only mass crime of the centuries and of course it is true that the Book of Job teaches man to accept without question all disasters, large and small. And yes, although the purists would like to keep the Holocaust a symbol and a word that applies only to Jews, I cannot help but feel that black slavery in America, Hiroshima and Stalin's Gulag also qualify as disasters so profound as to alter the colors of the universe forever. There are certain sickly hues, purples and ultraviolets, that are permanent parts of our internal landscape. Jew and Christian, we cannot forget, our lives have been devalued.

But at the mythological heart of it all (and I say mythological because the events, though real, have transmuted into symbolic and philosophical coin) is the experience of the Jews in Nazi-dominated Europe. That Holocaust has not yet sunk into the ages like the slavery of the Jews in Egypt—it remains a constant, open wound, a continuing sense of distrust of the political sanity of nations, a new knowledge of the potential for violence, destruction, sadism and, worst of all, depersonalization that may be in all of us. Rousseau's social contract and Locke's cheery blank page, all of society's declarations and edicts and laws, have proved fallible, and we can do no more than cower in our corners and hope that the places we have picked on earth to hide are safe. The Holocaust must have changed everything for Christians too. Their God of Mercy could not control the passions of His worshipers—centuries under His tutelage created disaster—the Christian way has proved itself to be no more than a Hallmark greeting card sent to a terminal cancer patient.

I want my stepdaughter's friend to understand but suddenly I am afraid of my own thoughts. We talk instead of Samuel Johnson, about whom he has knowledge and strong feelings. We talk about Hazlitt and Addison and Steele. We are all animated and happy. We belong after all to the same civilization—or almost the same civilization.

Rabbi Abraham J. Heschel writes that we Jews are messengers who have forgotten our message. If this is so, perhaps it explains why so many Jews have been killed and persecuted throughout history—perhaps the message we have forgotten contains bad news—perhaps of woes even larger than those now known. Bearers of evil tidings have traditionally been killed once their message has been received.

I am thirteen years old. My best friend's father, who was an orthopedist and worked generously in clinics in Harlem, has died suddenly of a heart attack. My childhood is over. I know it because the pictures of Dachau and Treblinka that were published in *Life* magazine are hidden in my closet.

I write volumes of atrocious poetry. I am beginning the shredded days of adolescence where yearning and exaggeration will make the simplest things painfully complex and the complex things subject to generalizations and arrogance. It is Yom Kippur morning. I tell my mother I am not going to temple. I am never going again. God is evil, I say. She stands at my door. Her eyes are swollen. They, my parents, the yin and yang of my universe who loathe each other and cannot leave each other, they have been fighting.

"Everyone will notice; they will talk if you don't come," she pleads.

I am indifferent. A few days earlier I had bought a copy of the *Daily Worker*. When I opened it at the dinner table, my father had screamed about pinkos and Commie spies, about treason and Rosenbergs. I hadn't minded the diversion. I didn't mind if the aunts and the uncles, the cousins and the cousins' cousins, talked about me.

"It's as easy to marry a rich man as a poor man," my mother had reminded me as I went off to dancing school the week before. I intended to marry a non-Jewish man in rags. I was then only at the beginning of my obnoxiousness.

———

Rabbi Jacob Neusner is a square, solid man who seems to suffer from no doubts, no tremors of irony, no whispers of second guesses and third possibilities. His voice is thunderous, rabbinical, and his manner is authoritative, bossy, somber and direct. Nothing twinkles, sparkles, shines in the corners of his mind. He makes me want to slip away, take my dogs and go for a long walk in the silent woods. He makes me want to be with women friends. But I admit there is a force, a patriarchal force, in his intellect. He writes: "The Jews see themselves as a group, though their group should have ceased to hold them when the faith lost its hold upon them and that is a paradox.

They see themselves as bound to others in other lands and other ages, whom they have never seen and with whom they have nothing in common but it is claimed—forefathers."

Blu Greenberg told me that although she is the daughter of an Orthodox rabbi, though she had lived her entire life as an Orthodox Jew, it was only when she was in the hospital, having given birth to her second son, whom she named David (now she had two sons, Moshe and David), did she feel a euphoria, that sense of being directly connected to the long line of Jewish history, of continuity. Now she felt she understood the purpose of being a Jew and what it meant in her life and in her children's lives. In the hospital she felt an overwhelming Jewish happiness textured with, and yet over and beyond, the normal happiness of bringing forth a healthy baby. Beyond being an assertion of Jewish family life this may also be a hint of the profound patriarchal nature of Judaism that it took not one but two male children before Blu Greenberg could fully feel the joy of history and family as they intersected in her life. Her euphoria, however, was real enough and her sense of connection is deep and unquestionable.

Rabbi Neusner, a man more determined than euphoric, goes on to say: "Jews see their history as one history though they are not everywhere involved in it. They reflect on the apocalyptic event of the day as intimately and personally important to them. They died in Auschwitz. They rose again in the State of Israel. They bear fears on account of the past, though that past is nothing to them except that it is the Jews. They have nightmares that belong to other men but are not within their personal experience at all except that they are Jews. They see themselves as brands plucked from burning, though they never stood near the fire. The classical faith demands that each man see himself as redeemed at Sinai from bondage to the Pharaoh."

All this is quite true. Rabbi Neusner feels this connection comes from the covenant God made with the Jews. I think it springs naturally from Jewish education which teaches these connections over and over and repeats them at every holiday and social occasion. There are many advantages to maintaining tribal memory and tribal time. How much more satisfying it was for Blu Greenberg to have her David and her Moshe within the flesh of Israel, to contribute to the living group destiny. How much better than being alone, a mother and her two sons, a dangling fragment of the fragile human experience emerging from oblivion and headed toward oblivion.

Rabbi Neusner: "Jews are all children of Abraham, Isaac and Jacob. Their forefathers stood at Sinai and bound them for all time and the terms of the contract were to do and hear the word of God. That covenant has never been broken. A Jew who does not keep the covenant still has its imprint engraved on his flesh. His children do not require conversion if they choose to assume its responsibilities. The world has understood the indelibility of the covenant for it has murdered the seed of Abraham into the third generation."

Although a child is considered Jewish if only its mother is Jewish, Rabbi Neusner refers only to he, him, and his . . . his forefathers, men and man. Perhaps this is a petty observation and yet it may also explain Blu Greenberg in her joy in her hospital bed.

———

My youngest daughter Becky had a close friend in the third grade who attended the Sunday school at St. James Episcopal Church on Madison Avenue in New York. They had a "bring a friend to church" program and Isabelle was always asking Becky to join her and I was always reluctant about the invitation even when it included lunch and a movie afterward. One day Becky and Isabelle had an argument. Isabelle said that there was a real heaven and hell and Becky said there was no such thing—that was just a story. Isabelle got red and angry.

Becky got stubborn and shouted. Then Isabelle suggested that they make a bet.

"It's not a fair bet," said Becky. "If you're right you'll be able to prove it and if I'm right I'll never be able to prove it because we'll just be dead."

The subject was dropped.

It's a good thing Darwin was right and Lamarck was wrong. If genes changed by mere usage, our children, male or female, would have fifty percent diminished wit by now. Women excluded so long from study would have become addlepated. Think of what did happen. Cynthia Ozick has pointed out that fifty percent of the possible scholars and students were lost to the Jewish community. Think what would have happened had half our gene pool adapted to the kitchen and the market.

That there are no atheists in foxholes is an old saw, probably older than foxholes themselves, but I thought my skepticism was like Arnold Schwarzenegger's stomach muscles: practiced, trained and invincible. Then last summer my daughter Kate developed a swollen knee. At first we were unconcerned and thought she had injured herself in some vague trauma, perhaps jumping rope or running. After several weeks during which the swelling did not subside and she seemed tired and at odds with the world, we went to New York for definitive tests. The symptom we knew could indicate a variety of severe and even fatal illnesses or it could be a milder assault. She had X rays and blood tests. All night long my husband and I lay rigid in the bed, awake and alone. Our individual terror, the directions of our imagined nightmares were too vivid for mutual comforting. During that time I was not angry with God for designing a universe that would so unjustly threaten a small child. I forgot my hatred of YHWH and the years of doubt that had encrusted my soul, and I began to beg, to plead, offering to exchange anything for her safety, promising never to write another word, and so forth. The onlooker within scoffed at this crawling performance but this was no time for reason or consistency. I was simply too frightened. The emergency passed. We were spared. I returned to my usual philosophical positions, somewhat altered by the knowledge that the existentialism of my college days was far more appealing when there were no stakes on the table—when one has no hostages to fortune. It is hard to believe in the laughter of the gods down the corridors of the galaxies as propounded by Hesse, Sartre, and others when one's own child is the butt of the joke.

I am twenty-six years old and in my first marriage. My mother had a small cancerous mole on her leg removed. She then had surgery on the lymph nodes in the groin and abdomen and half a year later she lay in bed in her apartment where I had grown up, under the silk coverlets, dying of a brain metastasis. The dying had been going on a long while. There was a private nurse who was knitting a sweater for her grandchild. My father took long walks up and down Park Avenue and made business calls from the study that had once been my room. My young daughter pulled a squeak toy across the marble hall floors. My brother came from medical school, my aunts came and went between their appointed rounds of dressmakers and hairdressers. Suddenly my mother, who had been unable to talk but whose consciousness was all too conscious, convulsed, vomited on her satin lace bed jacket and within minutes died. It was a relief for her, for us. Nevertheless, the long halls of the apartment had not seemed so hollow, so sterile, since I was a child listening to the sounds of my imagination corrupt the night. My grief was not free of ambivalence and my guilt for various matters of thought and deed mingled with a certain unbidden sense of liberation to create a psychological numbness that like most anesthetics did its work fairly well.

Someone called the funeral home. The doctor came and wrote a certificate. I took my daughter into the kitchen for lunch.

The doorbell rings. Cantor David Putterman from the Park Avenue Synagogue has come. He waits in the study to discuss the funeral plans with my father. He was the cantor there when I had attended Sunday school. He has a briefcase under his arm. He is clean-shaven. He looks like the tribe of stockbrokers, insurance salesmen, accountants who visited my mother in the past. His eyes are soft and puzzled. Now that I look carefully at his face I can see that he is a man of sensitivity and thought. I offer him some coffee. We wait as my father is on the phone notifying relatives of my mother's large family. The cantor has heard of me. He has seen one of my husband's plays off Broadway. He is very glad to have this opportunity to meet me. He takes from his briefcase something he has brought just for me—hoping that he would have the chance to speak with me. He rummages in his briefcase and finds the pamphlets he is looking for. He hands them to me. I scan the titles and the first and last paragraphs. Each one is a sermon by a different rabbi or theological professor on the evils of intermarriage. Two of the pamphlets are written for young couples planning to take such a treacherous step. They warn of high divorce rates, incompatibility because of different value systems, they describe the loneliness of young people whose families no longer include them in major events. Silently I am reading the pamphlets when there is an interruption. The men from Campbell's funeral home have come for the body. I am asked to choose a dress from the closet in which my mother will be buried. Standing among her clothes (she never felt she looked right, each dressing would take many false starts and groans of self-dislike), I felt a certain fear of the death that was in the house. A child's sense that there are terrors beyond words and they may lurk in closets. Quickly I pick a dress. The men wrap my mother in a black rubber sheet and carry her down the elevator, the back elevator. I return to the cantor and thank him for his pamphlets, explaining to him that since I am already married their contents are of limited use.

"You never can tell," he says in that sonorous voice of one for whom the words are all written out and he has only to repeat them at the right time to assure a wide and approving audience. I put the gaggle of reprint pamphlets in the drawer of a black Chinese lacquered desk. With such a wonderful sense of timing I wish that this cantor had been Saint Paul. It would have saved the Jews from centuries of anti-Semitism.

Several months later as my husband and I were ending a marriage that had lost (with our growth) its reason for being, and as he was packing his things and we were having civilized conversations about who got to keep the books and where the sofa should reside, I had a sudden impulse to ask him to unpack everything, to try again, to mend the irreparable. This impulse did not stem from any genuine nostalgia for what might have been or any fear of the future; the marriage was already an insubstantial shadow for both of us. My urge to replace his shirts in the drawer came from my irritation at letting that cantor have a victory—adding me to his statistics and probably saying some Hebrew form of "I told you so" around the synagogue. It was petty and childish of me I knew, but still it was not our different religious or ethnic backgrounds that caused us to separate. In matters of philosophy and theology we were harmonious beyond anything a computer could design. There were other reasons, compelling, urgent and private, for us to part.

Several years later I met the man who was to become my second husband. As we saw more of each other and the evening dates slipped into afternoons and mornings and our courtship built slowly toward its inevitable climax, I was furious that now, despite myself, I would be gratifying the cantor.

I believed that it was only an accident that this man was, in fact, Jewish. On the other hand I believed as a fledgling Freudian that there are no accidents of the emotional life. I was too old and worn to assume that ideology could affect my personal choices. I granted the cantor his victory although it really galled me to do it. Sometimes I do wonder if it was or was not coincidence, mere chance, or did my new love contain just a trace, a faint vapor of ethnic return? Impossible to tell.

On intermarriage . . . At first in Palestine the Jews intermarried freely. Often they brought their husbands' and wives' families into the tribe and enlarged it. But soon we read of the prophets coming out of their retreats and inveighing against the stranger. Now intermarriage was taking Jews away from their religion and exposing them to the idolatrous practices of neighbors. To marry within the tribe became very early an important, openly stated means of Jewish survival, and to create out of each person's marriage a double tying to the tribe became one of the major emotional threads of the religion.

Ezra, the famous royal scribe, dissolved by law in 458 B.C.E. all foreign matrimonial alliances. It staggers the mind to think of the suffering to parents and children, husband and wife, this edict must have produced. Many centuries later Christians dissolved marriages that had been made to Jews and forbade any Jew to marry a Christian. The issue of intermarriage had been joined, and ironically enough the bigotry of one group served to reinforce the tribalism of the other and the laws of Ezra (revealing a dangerous human rigidity) reached a far more dangerous form in the Nazi Nuremberg laws of 1936.

Blunting the attraction of the Jewish population for Hellenism must not have been an easy task. During the occupation of Trajan a Jewish band of terrorists, fanatics and patriots all, went into the hills and took to decapitating both parties of intermarriages on their wedding night: To these zealots the crime of assassination was nothing to the treason of intermarriage, which threatened the entire state, the body politic of the Jewish people.

The Romans themselves legislated against intermarriage with Jews from regime to regime, and the counts and barons and little princes of Europe would grant Jews charters to move within their domains, providing no intermarriages occurred. In the Middle Ages in Germany relationships between Jew and Christian were punishable by flogging, the galleys, or worse; but by the middle of the eighteenth century the proudest European nobility had often married a Jewish heiress (one person's social law is always another's irresistible temptation). In some areas mixed marriages were more numerous than the reverse. Within a few generations Jewish blood ran through many strata of society. The pull toward intermarriage has remained as strong as the pull toward separatism, and despite laws, prejudices, ghettos and other less visible barriers, people seem determined not to stay in their assigned places. If anti-Semitism has continually threatened the Jews and the very existence of the Jewish people, then intermarriage has been only a more benign form of threat—nibbling at, eroding, the population of the Jewish community wherever permitted.

The status of Jew as pariah (the reason for not wanting intermarriage on both sides was fear of disdain) was clearly marked by the Christian laws on intermarriage and often became the "legal" basis of the illegal acts of massacre and brutality that followed. However, who is the pariah and who is the member in good standing of the tribe is in the eye of the beholder. The Agudah (the right-wing Orthodox group in Israel) protested the peace treaty with Egypt and the opening of normal borders between countries. They gave as their reason for this opposition a fear that with open borders there would be an increase in intermarriage. It is also true that intermarriage reduces the actual numbers of the Jewish nation and threatens its survival as severely as the murderous persecutions of the past. Intermarriage is then a real threat to the body politic and feared as such. But the entire subject of intermarriage has become symbolic—mythologized—and caught in our most irrational and primitive fears.

My daughter Kate, still eleven years old, meets a young man named Amos at a school dance. Amos's mother and I talk on the telephone as the children plan to go to the movies.

"Amos asked me," she says, "if Kate was Jewish." Amos's mother laughed. "It's a big thing in our house," she adds.

"Yes," I say, "Kate is Jewish." I wouldn't want to give a little boy anxiety.

In the Sholem Aleichem story, Tevye, the father, mourns for his daughter as if she were dead because she married a Gentile. To leave the tribe, to cut oneself off from the family and the family history, is then to lose the world or to die (symbolically, at least). A friend who is Jewish describes the day his father closed his grocery store in Brooklyn and the whole family in their holiday outfits took the subway into Manhattan to go to the theater. Jacob Adler was playing Tevye on Second Avenue. At a crucial moment, midway through the second act, the stage was dark, there was a small candle burning, over which the father sat rocking back and forth in bitterness and grief, denying the life of the daughter who had abandoned him in abandoning her faith. The small boy could hear his own father's heavy breathing and saw his hands clenching the arms of the seat in shared agony with the actor on the stage. The small boy wondered, What if I should do that when I'm older, find a shiksa and be dead to my parents? The thought filled him with horror and at the same time opened a crack in the walls of his universe, promising freedom, a possibility of escape. Years later, when he was teaching English at a women's college and he married his French Catholic wife and his father's grief outshone Tevye's because it was more bitter and endured longer since it was real and not staged, he wondered if, after all, the direction had not been taken that day years earlier in the theater. That marriage has lasted over thirty-five years, with all the usual collections of grievances and guilts that do not give any particular insight or judgment into the nature of intermarriage.

My friend Ramona went to high school with me. She is the daughter of German Jews of some wealth and social aspirations. She had no religious training and her family's only real remaining link to Judaism was the name Birnbaum. Ramona told me that on one of her vacations home from Radcliffe, she was walking with her mother along Madison Avenue and looking in windows for a dress for a friend's coming out party. They passed a tall, blond young man with blue eyes and no nose to speak of, and Ramona turned to her mother and said, "I'm going to get one of those for myself." Several years later she did. He was the son of a prominent Boston family that had given this country Harvard deans, prep-school headmasters, ministers and poets. Ramona's family was delighted. But after the birth of her third child the young man, who turned out (as if life were a morality play) to be witless and characterless, ran off with an airline attendant and left Ramona with her visions of a safe harbor radically altered.

———

My nephew climbed to the top of a small slide when he was two years old. He looked around him, up at the sky and down at the waiting ground. "Oy vay," he called out and cautiously backed down the steps. Is this story evidence of our Jewishness? My nephew's for his world view and mine for laughing?

———

Psychoanalysis is considered by many to be a Jewish science. This is not quite true. Psychoanalysis as begun by Freud and unraveling even unto the human potential movement lays claims to certain universal, verifiable (through repetition) observations. What is true is that Jews have rushed to psychoanalysis as lemmings to the sea and of course—why not?—it seems logical. Out of the traditions of the pilpul, out of the rabbinical nervous busybody concern about all the little matters of human life from food intake to marital sexual habits to clothing and child rearing, the Jewish tradition of God and His rules mingling with the commonest of kitchen practices makes it easy for the modern mind to glide into psychoanalysis, where interpretation is made of all minor acts, thoughts, wishes, word slips, patterns of sex and love, and everything is seen, not as God's revealed law, but as the design of the unconscious shaping the personality. God was the regulator of all things and now man places himself as the investigator, the judge of the quality and nature of his daily life. Now man worries over the habits and individual mannerisms of his unconscious just as his rabbinical fathers worried themselves over the normative word. To attend any psychoanalytic conference is to think of the works of the Midrash, the commentaries of Rashi, the scholars of Gaon as they accumulated centuries of opinions on matters whose first assumptions might seem to outsiders rather bizarre. To see relevance in the most trivial and private matters of life is quite the ancient Jewish view: Separated from the concept of God this work goes on but is now performed in the service of humanism or the hope of freeing man to be his best. (That ideal of the Enlightenment lingers on in the twentieth century like just so much salt in our wounds.)

Psychoanalysis also contains the particularly Jewish experience of history in which the demonic, the aggressive, impulse rises up in each generation and tears apart the civilization at least on the Jewish side of the street. Jews have known a stream of demons: Egyptians, Syrians, Romans, Spaniards, Portuguese, Italian popes and petty princes, barons and Poles, cossacks and czars, Nazis and Stalinists, Turks and Iranians.

Freud reconceived this dramatic history—forging the link between the individual psychology of man and mass destiny. Freud saw history as recapitulated within the individual, a steady war of ego against primitive barbarism. Freud could view the violent impulses of men and women as natural.

Perhaps it took a Jewish genius to conceive of placing the historical reality of the Jewish experience inside the soul of man and explaining something of both.

The very form of the science is analogous to Jewish culture: After Freud made his early discoveries of the relevance of childhood sexuality and the powers of the unconscious, he set up a teaching program, a gathering of interested followers, as had the old rabbis of the early days after the destruction of the Second Temple. He met with the proselytes and the proselytizers, and just as existed in the great academies of Babylon, there grew splits and divisions. Freud made each person a torah unto himself and the rabbi doctors became the interpreters of the hidden patterns of the self.

Freud himself half-believed in a kind of messiah, a redemption that would be a long time coming. He had hopes that science would itself become the messiah and untie the knots of civilization and release men and women from their neurotic compulsions that had brought about so much suffering. This faith in the positive benefits of science was Freud's form of "next year in Jerusalem." Freud did worry that this might be another illusion, but then even the great rabbis of the Diaspora themselves doubted from time to time the coming of the Messiah.

Freud himself took on certain messianic attributes (just as the great rabbis have always done). Students flocked from all over the world to study with him. His letters and papers have been collected and annotated. After his death there has been among his followers a certain hardening of positions as if a sacred text had been written and it and its leaders sanctified. Was Freud the Sabbatai Zevi of the modern world? (Unfair comparison—glib and inaccurate—Sabbatai Zevi gave only false hope and brought disillusionment, while Freud has opened some windows and allowed new directions to be taken.) But it is true that among the followers, the interpersonal wonders, the best friends and the primal screams and the okay types among the neophytes and the analysands, much false hope and exaggerated promises have been exchanged. Too many people have sold everything, packed their bags and waited fruitlessly to be transported to a promised land.

The attraction of so many Jews to the practice and clinical experience of psychoanalysis may be because it enables them to combine the traditions of old forms of thinking while entering the modern world. By focusing on the universal psychology of mankind, the Jewish mind can remove the stigma of Jewishness, undo the sense of specialness and concentrate on the general and the common.

Why did I compare psychoanalysts to lemmings? (Not a very flattering comparison!) I think I only meant to capture the quality of herd compulsion, and after all most of us, like lemmings, are in the sea, however we got there. Our supports have turned liquid and toss us about in most ungentle ways. We share our environment, inner and outer, with things that are slippery, oozing, primeval and ferocious.

My brother, who is less of a romantic than I and not at all a hysteric (sins I admit), says the above is all nonsense. He points out that Jesuits are analytic thinkers, that the medieval world was filled with regulations and laws about daily matters, that obsession and compulsion are the bedrock of all religious forms. The explanation he gives for the preponderance of Jews in psychiatry is that medicine itself attracts and has historically attracted large numbers of Jews way out of proportion to their numbers in the community. (Another example of Jewish humanism—Jewish concern for others.)

"Look at a list of the names of cardiologists or radiologists," my brother says. "No one has ever suggested that cardiology is a Jewish science, but then cardiology lacks its Woody Allen."

I'm fortunate that I can hold two opposing opinions in my mind at once because my brother has a very good point.

There were many Columbia students and their girlfriends hanging around the West End bar on Upper Broadway in the late 1950s. The Zeitgeist (and we did talk a lot about Zeitgeist, a word that seems to have dropped from my vocabulary) was coated with the fallout from logical positivism, about whose precise practice I had only vague inklings but whose implications seemed clear enough. We talked a lot about Sartre and about Camus, whose picture (cut from the back of a *Playbill*) was posted above my bed for reasons less philosophical than I would like to admit. We understood the myth of Sisyphus as the exact allegorical model for human guilt and punishment. We saw ourselves rolling stones up and down mountains without relief, without purpose, for sins we never comprehended or selected. We saw the end as oblivion and the road as absurd.

All that despair did not significantly diminish our long, amiable drinking evenings together. Among us were several Korean War veterans who, although white, affected the black slang, making them seem particularly entitled to the darkest despair. We were beyond politics because all isms had already shown their bloody feet. We were beyond or before protest because we saw none around us and we felt an inevitability to the historic process that made us seem like a cluster of flies at dusk. Our perspective on human history was so broad, so grand, that we suffered from altitude enervation.

The atomic bomb hung over our heads. It seemed inevitable that in our lifetime, an accident, a sudden onset of psychosis, would send something across a radar barrier and bring us all to a swift and deserved end. Personally we were cool. Our poets quoted Baudelaire and *J. Alfred Prufrock*. Our playwrights recited paragraphs from Beckett, our sculptors doodled abstract gravestones for mass graves on the cocktail napkins served with each beer. We sat on barstools making gallows humor jokes in the middle of the Cold War as befits those who take their own postures seriously. Sometimes we behaved as if Auden were looking at us. We wanted not so much to save ourselves as to be clever in the interim. If we had only known the sixties were coming, if we had only known the sexual revolution was at least a mote in Masters' and Johnson's eye, we might have breathed a little easier.

None of this had anything to do with being Jewish. Jewish had disappeared from my mind along with the swimming pool at the country club I no longer visited. Being Jewish had evaporated from my mind along with the last of my segregated Jewish dancing classes (my last hope of attracting what my mother saw as a suitable mate from a good family). As my black leotard and sandals demonstrated, I was a citizen in good standing of bohemia, of beatnik turf. I thought of myself as tribeless, stateless, countryless, classless, religionless. My crowd suffered deep nostalgia for Paris of the twenties. We sprinkled our conversations with quotes from Gertrude Stein and Rainer Maria Rilke. We were free citizens in a world we thought would soon end in a whisper.

The thought of trying to explain this state of mind to Gluckel is horrifying. I think even if I had a large bank account she would not have wanted me to marry one of her sons.

My brother, four years younger, gifted at languages and music, had spent some of his early teens involved in Judaism. He had rebelled against the then bland, rich Park Avenue Synagogue and found his own synagogues where the learning was more serious and the culture more Jewish, more tied to the Old World shtetl. It was an odd rebellion, one that took his mind on interesting voyages to the study of Hebrew, Yiddish and Arabic. My father in his Brooks Brothers suit was not totally easy with his son who had journeyed into the Bronx to find what had been left behind on another continent. Eventually my brother drifted away—toward Proust and Thomas Mann and modernism—and he became a doctor and a scientist and a rationalist with a wry and sharp humor. But the Yiddishkeit remains. It insulates him against the logic of his mind. Without the protection of centuries of rabbinical jokes, a culture that was anchored so securely within the body of one group of people, within one legend, philosophical and scientific thought tends to give cold chills and bad hangovers.

Since I have begun to work on this book I have seen the extent of Jewish learning that I don't have. I have made desperate efforts to browse through the centuries, tasting samples here and there and gathering new vocabulary and at least a general view of the geography. I can never be more than a visitor, like a tourist at an Oriental bazaar quite exhausted by the strange sights and smells and sounds. Some nights I list for myself the ignorances that prey on me. I don't know the Torah, the Talmud, the words of Rabbi Hillel, the works of Maimonides or the volumes of Josephus, or Judah ben Samuel Halevi or the words of Rabbi Akiba. I know the meaning of Halakah, but beyond the simplest ideas of kashruth (dietary laws) and personal cleanliness I am vague. I do not know exactly what is lawful and what is not and what laying t'fillin (phylacteries) is exactly and what obligations of prayer and ritual are required beyond the keeping of the Sabbath. I don't speak either Hebrew or Yiddish. I am a provincial, caught in a modern time, a prisoner perhaps of limited education. I am pressing my nose flat against the glass, watching the consumption of a "prepared feast." The more time I spend in the Judaica room at the Forty-second Street public library, the more diminished I feel. However, there are certain ironies that must be noted. This very respect I have for languages, learning, scholarship, did not come from my Jewish parents, for whom financial gain was wisdom itself. It came from my Christian school, my secular college.

On the bus home from the library I make a list of the things I know at least slightly. This is a defensive maneuver but I find it comforting. I begin with the Russian novels and Occam's razor and Bishop Berkeley, the conjugation of the Latin word amo. My list is short, random, and finally I realize I should study it all again but I haven't time and I haven't strength and one really only has a few chances to culture oneself and after that it's all improvisation until death.

I regret my lack of Jewish learning but am not discouraged (or only temporarily) from continuing to explore the question of American Jewish identity. After all, there are many of us assimilated Jews from the learningless classes of the Jewish world. I am a journalist and as such I am expected to be a voyeur.

It is purported to be Jewish to love scholarship. Every Jew, in telling you why they are proud of being Jewish, speaks about the Jewish love of learning. Of all the Jews I talked with as I was writing this book, most had rabbi scholar grandfathers, fathers or famous theologist uncles. In the Warsaw ghetto just before the Nazis closed in, small groups of plumbers and carpenters would hire a student or a scholar to teach them during their lunch hours. On the Lower East Side, if one is to believe all the reports, which must have been coated with some nostalgia and prettifying, the streets were paved with books, political lectures and poetry series. Philosophical speakers could fill halls with tired workers who thirsted for knowledge. Sometimes they would fall asleep on the hard chairs after their ten-hour workday.

In Paris one summer late in the 1950s I met a young American who had spent the winter in Finland on a Fulbright scholarship. He told me, as we sat in the Café au Deux Magots where Sartre sometimes came, that he hated Jews. He had grown up in Brooklyn and gone to Peter Stuyvesant, a special high school for talented students. In those days they seated the

classes in order of academic rank. In the back were the Catholic boys. In the middle were the Protestant, and the front
three rows were all the kikes, or so he said. He made a sour
face telling me this. His anger was real enough, but I laughed
with pleasure. I felt increased—smarter myself because, after
all, it was my gene pool that had won the first desks. But I remind myself now, learning is not genetically determined, like
the color of one's eyes. And in fact I have known a lot of very
stupid Jews who have been left behind in the American race
for money and glory and excluded from the pride of learning
by certain densities of wit. Not everybody's father was a rabbi.
The fools of Chelm traveled to America too. It must have been
the smartest thing they ever did. It took a writer as angry as
Mike Gold to write in his classic *Jews Without Money* of the
prostitutes and the gangsters and the Jewish lowlife that
crawled about Delancey Street along with scholars and poets,
the readers of Dickens and Trotsky, and the old pious men.

On Thanksgiving of 1979, the turkey sits, browned, steaming
in its juices. The cranberries are already on the table. The
sweet potatoes and marshmallows rest on the counter waiting
for their moment. The table is decorated with the leftover
treasures from my mother's house. The finer things are
chipped. The lace tablecloth has burn holes hidden under salt
shakers and candlesticks. The gold leaf has worn off the Viennese glasses but there is still a certain grandeur to it all, no mis-
taking it for the Thursday before or the Thursday after. The
smaller children have made place cards with pictures of turkeys
and Pilgrims and Indian feathers. Our guests have brought
flowers and homemade bread. We have all worked hard, chopping, stirring, peeling for the last two days. We have four kinds
of pie ready for dessert. We have creamed onions, chestnut
stuffing and string beans. We are all dressed up; even Becky,

who prefers her stable boots to velvet, didn't argue about wearing a dress.

We sit down to dinner, but before we eat, we read. Each member of the family, each of our guests, reads a poem of his/her choice. We go around the table by order of birth, youngest to oldest. I almost always read Gerard Manley Hopkins, "Glory be to God for dappled things . . . all things counter, original, spare, strange." I choose this poem not so much to give glory to God but rather because I feel so dappled myself. Emily Dickinson, Robert Frost, Rod McKuen, Bob Dylan, Wallace Stevens, Edgar Allan Poe and Jack Kerouac are among the selections. Each year the poems are different but always consistent with the reader, something personal the reader wants to say to the gathering in this indirect way; the poem marks the moment in the reader's life and it is shared with family and friend. After we read, we eat. At the end of the cleaning up I am always exhausted, empty somehow; it's been good but never quite good enough. That defines it as a holiday, doesn't it?

There are contradictions and ambivalences in our celebrating Thanksgiving. We are recent Americans. It wasn't the Mayflower that brought our people over here. We know too much about what the coming of the white men did to the Indian and therefore the sweet pictures that the children draw of Pilgrim and corn provoke other images of Indians dying of smallpox, of massacres at Wounded Knee and treaties broken and violated. We can hardly say the word "American" itself without apologizing to the black slaves who didn't ask to come here and the Japanese at Hiroshima who were burned beyond the necessities of war, the Vietnamese, the Cambodians, certain members of the Chilean Left, some students in countries in the Third World; the inhabitants of the South Bronx and Bedford-Stuyvesant and Watts and on with a list of sorrows; a falling short of ideals that is enough to make any descendant of the original Mayflower cover his/her face with shame.

And yet we are very American. We have grafted ourselves

to Thanksgiving (even though my husband first heard of the holiday in a Flatbush public school). We have grafted ourselves to Halloween, to July Fourth picnics, and on Easter we give our children bunnies and jelly beans. We, after all, speak the language of Johnny Carson, of Dunkin' Donuts, of General Motors and IBM. In this country my husband received fourteen more years of education than his father. His world is more than fourteen times wider, broader, more comfortable and more challenging. As children in American schools we were taught the values and virtues of democratic ideals; a little later we learned how far we were from realizing those ideals, but still, even with all the tarnish, all the hard-earned skepticism, we have left some small light of hope in the democratic process—in the New World. How could we not? Nothing terrible has happened to us here yet. We have grafted ourselves onto the American body and we can only hope that there is no autoimmune process that will reject us, no surprise (such as experienced by German and Italian Jews) to confront our children or our grandchildren.

In the meanwhile we teach the children that they are American and that as Americans they are represented by the Constitution and the Declaration of Independence and we take them to visit historic Puritan villages and we make much of Abraham Lincoln and Martin Luther King, Jr. At Thanksgiving we are grateful that the first settlers survived to plant crops, to harvest and multiply. (Of course, I don't entirely forget that the descendants of that first supper are the ones who wouldn't admit my pediatrician, Dr. Samuel Solomon, into most medical schools, and that the quotas on Jews everywhere in American life were imposed by the relatives of the fine Pilgrim people husking the corn by the dawn's early light.) I have today bought chocolate turkeys for the children and a Pilgrim hat made of cardboard hangs on the front door, and bunches of Indian corn decorate the coffee table. I don't forget a single symbol. (Is that a sign of a "nouveau American"?)

This year I noticed for the first time that the family custom (invented in the first days of a second marriage) of reading poetry aloud at the table one by one reminded me of the Seder readings of my childhood when the Haggadah was passed around the table and was read section by section. Is this poetry reading (also before being permitted to eat) a recreation, a melding of childhood holiday into our adult nonaligned life? Have we declared all of literature our sacred text? (From Boccaccio to John Denver, man's comments, not God's actions, are the subject of our readings.) Have we then turned the American Thanksgiving into a kind of secular Seder, a pass over from the worship of God to the substitution of art? As each member of the family and our guests take their turn reading a poem, we can see that reverence for man's creativity replaces devotion to God. I am wondering if we have found a new form of piety or if our little ceremony is merely a pathetic attempt to create substance, echoes of tradition in a home where the spiritual bareness may be only too apparent.

Psychoanalysis, the medical specialty of my husband, is far more in our house than a mere hot water bottle for the pains of the spirit. I have been analyzed also and cannot imagine myself stripped of the personal insight and the ethics and culture of psychoanalysis. I cannot begin to think who or what I would be if I were without my own analysis and the comfort and company of my psychoanalyst friends and husband. Their conversations, their meetings, their papers form the intellectual scaffolding of my life. None of us except transsexuals can imagine ourselves totally without gender or completely within another gender. I've forgotten the generalizations, the first principles that represented my thinking before fifth grade, before I read The Catcher in the Rye, before I had heard of Dorothy Parker, before I had seen a Rothko or read The New Yorker. In just that way the experience of being analyzed be-

86

comes a coloration, a shaping, a part of one's education whose removal (some magic erasing) would alter in profound ways the specificity of self.

Psychoanalysis, whatever the doctors themselves may claim, carries a distinct ethical system, not, of course, separate from Judeo-Christian tradition, but a variant of its own. Without direct preaching (God forbid) from the analyst, the analysand picks up, intuits, absorbs these ethics, and they remain like sinew and muscle, part of the self—or the frame of the self. The first principles of these ethics have to do with the value, the extraordinary value, the doctor puts on the worth of each mind that comes before him. If one spends three, four, five hours a week with a patient, struggling with her/him in the darker recesses of her/his personal history to recover and un-cover the trivia of small pains and cumulative damage, me-andering through little blindnesses and tiny details of eating habits and sleeping skills, well, then, the spending of that time itself is an ethical statement. It gives to each human life a precious weight, attention is paid in ways exactly counter to the mass-produced, technological, assembly-line selves that much of the modern world tells us we are and should be con-tent to be. Analysts may see three hundred patients in a life-time. Each encounter is sanctified through the sense of value the doctor gives to the person who has sought help. True, only a capitalist, consumer society could permit so much to be given one individual, so much time, thought, effort for the elusive goal of one person's increased happiness. But economics aside, psychoanalysis is a therapy that assumes individual human worth. By definition, a totalitarian society would find its true practitioners of psychiatry subversive.

An ethical system, a moral way of responding to personal problems, business problems, was traditionally part of the rabbi's wisdom. It fell on his shoulders to arbitrate disputes, to grant divorce, to create peace between neighbors. Rabbis, ministers and priests still consider themselves guardians of ethics. Their teachings lead to the morally good life. Without the text of the rabbi to guide, I suspect that psychoanalysis has provided the replacement for an ethical way in my life. Breathing the air of the psychoanalytic culture forces certain conclusions that either are in themselves moral positions or lead directly to certain other moral conclusions that affect both behavior and attitude.

Things I have learned from my psychoanalysis:

1. The importance of biology, that is, drives, instincts, oral needs, sexual urges. Biology is not, as I had been brought up to believe, something to be ruled, subdued, controlled by law, repressed, ignored, despised, regretted and rejected in favor of virtues of the spirit. Biology (genital feelings, maternal feelings, toilet needs, body odors) should be welcomed, understood, admired, integrated with the other needs of life in a rational balance. Biology (menstruation, masturbation, conception, blowing your nose, intercourse) must be allowed as friend not enemy.

2. Work is one of the two pillars of life, proof of one's sanity, mark of one's success in belonging to the human community. Work and mastery of tasks are the basic components of internal harmony. The function of the self (work) in relationship to others is in and of itself an ethical good, a goal, the end result of mental health, an ethical absolute. Work, not because God willed it after the expulsion from Eden, work, not because idleness is sin or permits the devil to have his victories, but work, because without it the eyes of men and women lose sharpness and focus. Work creates the distance between us and the abyss. It protects us from perceiving too clearly our "equality with the oyster" (David Hume). Work prevents and precludes massive anxiety; work is the best barrier against fear.

3. The infinite complexity of the simplest human thought or action. Brain waves that constitute thought are loaded with levels of meaning, causes, patinas of the personal past and echoes of the unconscious or the repressed. The incredible, beautiful cellular structure of the dream, the unconscious mo-

tives of a particular telephone call, the choice of menu for dinner, the slip of a word, the shape of a gesture, make a unity, a whole fabric in which the patterns, although not clear to the conscious eye, are formed and reformed. This existence of pattern in relationship, in choices, in thoughts, is the aesthetic of psychoanalysis. Observing, interpreting the pattern, gives aesthetic pleasure. There is a kind of ecstasy in discovering order in what had first appeared random or coincidental.

4. Freedom is almost an empty word and its use fogs the mind, but when one thinks of small degrees of liberty from compulsions, phobias, obsessions, repetitions of past mistakes, freedom from self-inflicted cruelties or actions that harm others and enforce guilt and isolation or loneliness, these are hard-won accomplishments. They are not political in the broad sense, not really communal or exportable, but freedoms nevertheless, places where the human being may achieve a certain level of triumph, a minor portion of happiness: a worth, a good, an ultimate ethical good.

5. The patient identifies with the analyst who is concentrating so hard at any given hour on understanding the presenting soul. The patient absorbs the act of empathy and learns to imitate it. Empathy is the tool for balancing the individual need against the needs, wishes, hopes of others. The caring doctor indirectly teaches patients to listen and to care for others, to respect and expect in others the same peculiarities that have become apparent in the self.

Psychoanalysis did not make or invent a system of ethics. It springs of course from Judaism and Christianity and it blends no small amount of Aristotelian wisdom into the pot. Balance and moderation are after all the Greek model for what psychoanalysis calls "maturity." (Like all moral systems its essence is identical to all the others and yet it has a flavor, a tone, all its own.)

It is the last hour of my analysis. The small Greek sculptures that decorate the bookshelf are tinged with streaks of late afternoon sunlight. The smell of hyacinth rises from the row of green plants on the back table. My pulse is running hard. My smile is wan. His smile is sad. There were unfortunate limits to the extent of the travels we took. Every insight exposes new imperfections, more questions without answers. The love I felt for him, was of course an illusion, like the refraction of the proverbial oar in the water. Insight is a gift that heals and wounds or wounds and heals depending on the grace of the moment. The more knowledge I have won in this strange encounter the more puzzling the mystery. I have loved him—a love that echoed older loves, made them visible, exposing their cruel limitations, their dangling ends, my exasperating mistakes. I have loved him, illusion or not, and as I turn to go, closing the door behind me, I leave my notebook with the leather cover at the foot of the couch. As I walk down the stairs I make promises to myself never to forget, even as I start to forget, the shape of the face, the movement of the arm, the tone of voice. By the time I reach the corner I have turned my attention to the day ahead and to the one after that.

I am in the airport lounge waiting for the delayed plane that will take me to the First World Infant Psychiatry Conference being held in Portugal. I have just read in a Jewish history book that after the catastrophic earthquake in Portugal in 1755, Europe saw the last of the auto-da-fé. Did they think the earthquake was a divine comment? If so, why so late? My husband is leaving from Boston, so I am alone among the doctors reading through the program of the meeting, thumbing the pages of the papers they will deliver. Outside the heavy rain and mist smear the moving lights of trucks and cars, of planes lumbering like golems in the slippery darkness. The stationary lights cast their rays on the black ground—a thousand moons on a prehistoric lake. I look carefully at the doctors. The woman and the men alike are earnest and gray, bearing themselves with sobriety, like deacons of a Calvinist church uncertain of their own salvation. They all look like doctors: a certain control, a shared caution of people who know the worst, expect to accomplish little, but for reasons of routine, habit, education, income and irrational hope continue in the direction they have started. If only it were possible to understand this elusive matter of personality development: mother-child interaction, object relations, separations, omnipotence, drive organization, anal and oral levels, symbiosis, depression, aggression, fetish and on with the words that can describe a human destined for a life of pain before he/she has reached a height of three feet. In this lounge ninety percent of the doctors are Jewish. Fifty percent of them have European accents. They are trying to understand the mystery of unhappiness and unravel its origins down to the first moments of life. They aspire to so much and change so little. Is that perhaps what Jews have been chosen for?

———

Martin Bergmann, Ph.D., is a psychoanalyst from Prague. His father was a famous Hebrew scholar and a philosopher and his grandfather was a famous rabbi. Martin is in his sixties and his white hair almost reaches to his neck. His glasses slip forward when he gets excited and his suits seem always to be moving in a different direction than he is. He sits in his Fifth Avenue apartment surrounded by art objects he and his wife have brought back from trips to India and Japan. We are eating Viennese pastry with our coffee. Martin reaches to a shelf of leather-bound books and taking down a slim volume shows me his father's gymnasium autograph book with a few words of casual friendship written in German by classmate Franz Kafka. I hold the book in my hands. I stare at the small script letters. Kafka was a boy in knickers who signed yearbooks, of course and not of course. I hand back the treasure. I have nothing to offer in return to Martin, no connections with sanctified poets or artifacts of history. I have only my naked curiosity. I ask Martin to tell me about the Prague of his childhood. Instead he tells me about his sentimental voyage home a few Augusts earlier, his first return since he had fled the Nazis. He goes to the park where his nursemaid took him as a small child. He remembers her sitting on the bench with the grocer's assistant fondling her large breasts. A screen memory, of course, but only he knows what lies behind the screen. He tells me about the statue in the park and pigeons that he remembers eating bread crumbs from his hands.

Then he tells me of going to the Jewish cemetery in Prague. It is on the left. On the right is a well-kept neat Christian cemetery. New flowers mark recent graves, and visitors stroll on ordinary paths. In the Jewish graveyard there is obviously no tender of the plots, no gardener. There is no Jewish community in Prague for the first time in eight centuries. There is nobody's dim-witted cousin to take the job, no one to pay any continual respect to the dead and no newly overturned soil. This, after all, is a graveyard for single burials, not a site of mass interment. There are weeds and brush everywhere. The stones are tilted and covered with dirt and fungus. Only one grave has a clean path cut to it. Only one grave is pruned and the stone swept and the marker free of parasites and mold. This grave is a tourist attraction and kept up by the Communist state willing to finance the celebrity of this particular Jewish dead. This grave Martin comes to and can easily read the name: Franz Kafka.

Martin is older now than his grandfather was when he died. Martin pushes away the sticks and vines and moves slowly by ancient memory to the burial site of his grandfather, the one who gave him Hebrew lessons before he had learned to read in any other language. The grandfather who spoke five languages had no way of knowing that his grandson would grow up and become a doctor whose patients would speak only English. Martin remembers his grandfather because he sent him a weekly present for his stamp collection. Each Monday the little boy waited for the mailman to bring him his gift, and quickly he would rush to his room and paste the stamp into his album. The album is now in his office on Fifth Avenue in New York. In the jungle of the Jewish cemetery, Martin stumbled over the stone that marked his grandfather's burial place. The stone fell over, crashing into the weed and brambles. Martin felt an urgency to return the stone to its proper position. He squatted on the ground and pulled and pushed at the heavy granite with the Hebrew inscription, with his grandfather's name on it. He is not an unusually strong man. He has not taken to this American passion for physical exercise. His glasses fell off and he groped awhile to find them in the thickets under his feet. He pushed himself to continue, compelled by the forces of memory, a sense of order and dignity that he had learned as a child. He pulled at the stone like a man possessed, plagued by a host of memories of the man who would not recognize him, a man who was now only bones under the ground, a man who sent his grandson precious stamps. He sweated in the summer sun and removed his jacket. He opened his tie and wiped his glasses clear. He braced his toes against the rocks and branches at his feet. The stone stood straight up. It was erect and steady and the sunlight played on it and he leaned across to brush gently at the dirt that had accumulated in the lettering.

The stone crashed again backward onto the ground. Now it was hard to see exactly where it had been originally placed, where he had stood as a boy at the unveiling, holding his father's hand. His own father, long since buried in Israel, had then said the mourning prayers. Martin tried again to lift the stone. He embraced it and pulled; now his strength was gone and his passion was spent. He stood up and brushed off the dirt and the twigs and the briars from his pants. He retrieved his jacket from the stones on which it lay. Walking over the dead, striding on fallen markers, Martin walked out of the Jewish cemetery in Prague. After all, to whom did it matter,

93

the position of his grandfather's stone? His grandfather was not there to feel the offense. His grandfather had no mind to mind the neglect or the disrespect and Martin himself was the only one alive who could recall the old man's face and voice and he too was old. When he died, there would be no one who would recognize the name on the marker. It made no difference that the stone was down; the last visitor was just leaving. From the Christian cemetery came the strong smell of freshly cut grass.

The other guests were gone from the table. They were having coffee and brandy in the living room.

In Tomar, Portugal, where we had traveled after the First World Infant Psychiatry meetings, we go visit the Synagogia advertised on our tourist map. It is located down a wonderful, narrow cobblestone street. Canaries in small cages hang on the walls outside the small shuttered windows and sing back and forth to each other. The silver knockers on each tiny door are in the shape of a perfect miniature hand. The colors of the walls are white and pink and beige and raspberry and there are tiles above the doorposts picturing grapes and deer and flowers and hunters with bows and arrows. We find the synagogue but the door is locked. A sign in three languages tells us to ring the bell on a nearby building for the key. We do it. Down comes an old man who speaks just a little English. He opens the door of the synagogue for us. It was built in the 1200s, he says. We step across the threshold into a small, empty room with bare stone pillars leading up to a high arched ceiling. The empty room smells damp and feels like a mausoleum. There are no chairs, no pews, no Ark to house the Torah, no Torah at all, no stained-glass windows, no windows at all. Along the side of the wall have been arranged tombstone fragments with Hebrew writing on them, pieces found in abandoned castles, in graveyards or by the side of hidden roads in the south. A typed sheet explains in English and French that these stones were found by various archaeologists and sent to Tomar for safekeeping. We walk around silently in the empty room, like a crypt, like an empty skull.

"The Jews of Tomar," we ask the old man in French and in English, "how many are there now, and where do they worship?"

"All gone, all gone," he says. "Conversos," he shakes his head sadly, "converso." He shrugs. That's life, isn't it? What can an old man do who himself has always been a good Catholic and never personally forced anyone to change his/her religion himself. He smiles at us. He hopes we do not hold it against him that Emmanuel married the Infanta from Spain and she wouldn't consummate the vows until all Portugal was rid of Jews. We stand awkwardly in the late afternoon sunlight coming through the still open door. We tip him for his trouble. How long, after all, did it take him to secure this civic post? How many years of local political allegiance to the right people, or did he have a son-in-law at city hall? Anyway, we tipped him.

Converso is a euphemism for the farce, the burnings and the beheadings and the sealing up in the side brick walls and the baptisms by sword and the following massacres of "New Christians" at Easter time and plague time and in between times. It was in the year 1497 that the forced baptisms and exodus began, and shortly afterward the Inquisition held its autos-da-fé in the main square of Tomar.

At home neither my husband nor I would normally enter a synagogue filled with people, Torahs, cantors, rabbis, carpeting, soft lights. We had left the synagogue years ago, only to return when a friend's child is Bar Mitzvahed and we feel an obligation, one that usually evokes both nostalgia and irritation. We have left the synagogue, so why does this visit to an empty building in a small foreign town leave us with a certain hurt—a definite anger that spoils somewhat the architectural grandeur of the local monastery. We go on to see this monastery of the Knights Templars of Tomar. Its huge splendor mocks the little Synagogia, and while we, of course, admire the masonry and the intricate manueline columns, we do not find any moral sanctity wafting down the old halls. Despite the afternoon sun, the pleasure of being away together, the delight in the new and the unknown, the wine and cheese and the sea bisque, we cannot shake a certain bitterness. *Converso*—a deceit that leaves us uneasy.

Arthur Abraham has written a story called "The Testament of a Martyr." I found it in a book, *The Jewish Caravan*, collected by Leo Schwartz. The martyr is a man named Simon Morata who writes on the eve of his execution by the Spanish Inquisition. He tells of his fear of the Christian mob, of his unwillingness to flee the country and leave the grave of his wife. He describes seeing the beheading of a Jewish man. He describes his fear and his secret life as a Jew. He writes: "Although I might try to seek out some justification for my conversion, deep in my innermost self it seemed to me that the gift of life was but a sad reward for the harsh rumblings of conscience and the loss of my own self-esteem." Simon is tortured and refuses to reveal the reason he stayed in Spain. He does not want them to desecrate the grave of his wife. He writes of the torture. "I close my eyes and before them a world of red color reels round and round, and then deep darkness descends. I see no more, I hear no more, but feel the froth bubbling from my lips. Sense slowly returns and with it a question rushes into my mind. Is it possible, I ask myself, that these devils were children once?"

One cannot read this as ancient history or simple fiction. There are sides to be taken and consequences for taking them.

An anti-Zionist advertisement in *The New York Times* is placed by the Orthodox followers of the Satmar rabbi, Rabbi Yoel Teitelbaum. They consider the establishment of a Jewish state a blasphemous act that has been condemned by the Torah sages. They believe that Jews should "quietly await the coming of the true Mosiech." They consider the Zionists "not liberators of Eretz Yisroel but an occupation force." Oh, what compromising romantics these men are. We have already had too many dead students of Talmud and Torah who have missed the political dimensions of survival—of living or dying within the twentieth century . . . like a school of eyeless fish swimming toward a predator's mouth. This blindness arises naturally after centuries of living without political power; isolated from the real governments of their temporary abodes and treated always as pariahs and untouchables, their political sense has atrophied. On the other hand perhaps we with all our smart campaign talk, our political cynicism and sophistication (at least we are concerned with who has the power and why), will move directly toward a nuclear accident —a disaster we couldn't avoid even if we could see it coming— maybe it's just as well to be dreaming away in the twelfth century, but I'm not ready to do so yet.

In the Hotel Estoril Sol's coffee shop I talk with Dr. Anna Ornstein. She is a psychoanalyst from Cincinnati who is presenting a paper at the conference. She and her husband are both survivors of Auschwitz. I see the tattoo on her bare arm. She tells me that the day she got the tattoo was a happy one. She was convinced they would not kill her if they went to the trouble of the tattoo. She thought the number protected her from the gas chamber. She is originally from a small town in Hungary where there were only forty Jewish families. The native population had always been deeply anti-Semitic. They called names, they threw objects and taunted the Jewish children. They passed local laws forbidding Jews to be in certain parts of the town. The Jewish families formed their own subcommunities and developed a sense of moral superiority. After all, says Dr. Ornstein, "We had education, we had the Talmud, we had our intellects. We developed a sense of superiority that protected us from becoming identified with the aggressor. This defensive superiority helped us to endure the humiliations of those days."

Anna Ornstein was sixteen years old when she was deported to Auschwitz. She was strong enough to work, and although at one point she fell ill with a raging typhoid fever, she managed to survive the eighteen months in camp. Her father and brothers were all killed in a labor camp. After the war she and her husband went to Heidelberg to study medicine. She had been tutored by her mother at home for most of her highschool years and was able to pass the entrance exams. She and her husband came to America to obtain further training in their field and eventually became psychoanalysts, professors at a medical school and the parents of three children, the owners of a house in the suburbs, joggers, skiers, writers of papers, eager consumers of life, passionate supporters of Israel, leaders of a therapy group for survivors' children.

Anna Ornstein wants to tell me her story. She wants to talk about Auschwitz. She says it is important to bear witness. As she talks her eyes blaze and occasionally they fill with tears. I am embarrassed. I apologize for my questions.

"No," she says, "feeling is good. Each Passover I write another short story to be read at the table about my experiences in the camp. I want the children to know. Numbness is the danger; talking about it, feeling it, that is part of the healing."

The waiter brings us our coffee. It's nearly time for Anna to go back to the psychoanalytic meetings. She is chairing the afternoon session. I am guilty that my life has been so unthreatened. I am ashamed to have been a Jewish American. I am ashamed that I have fatigues and sometimes depressions, that I have in fact a smaller life flame than one who has so much more reason than I to have lost connection. I, who have none of her pain, also have none of her accomplishments.

Anna Ornstein speaks with special pride of her Jewishness. "My father talked about Lenin, Marx, Trotsky, Herzl. At home at the dinner table when I was a child everything was discussed and argued. That was part of our Jewish heritage. In the camps we didn't have the exact dates, we had lost track of time. But we celebrated the Holy Days anyway. We declared them from time to time. We who were starving still fasted. They could not deprive us of our Judaism. The holidays gave us strength. We Hungarian Jews were better off than the Italian Jews. The Italians didn't know they were Jewish. I saw a trainload of Italian women come into Auschwitz, after the haircuts, after the showers. The Germans took everything away from them as usual, but they left them their high-heeled shoes. In panic and in rage, they started to fight with one another, using their shoes as weapons. They hurt each other badly. We were better prepared emotionally. That is why we would never have done that—in the boxcars we shared the cracks of air, we exchanged leaning space, we took turns and helped the sicker and weaker ones. Strangely the anti-Semitism in Hungary prepared us. We had learned that our Judaism was not merely a negative that had caused this horror."

I asked Anna Ornstein, whose work was rational and scientific, why she had remained involved with the Jewish traditions of her childhood, why did she pass them on with such emphasis and underlining to her children (who she proudly told me had wanted to be with one another on the Passover holiday)?

"We Jews," she had answered, "are molded together like a family; because of our incredible and unique history we have developed our own intellectual modes, the modes of logic and humor that we share with other Jews. We are a single family that traces its history back to before the Flood. Being Jewish is one of the major ingredients of my psyche. I could not live suspended in air. I need my roots, my feelings of belonging. I can be a part of the Jewish people without accepting all of its religious positions as absolute truths."

At the farewell dinner of the analytic meetings in Portugal, I see Anna in a brilliant red dress on the dance floor. She is a superb dancer and men of all ages are watching her, admiring the sheer energy, the vibrations of sex and pleasure she molds into the dance. The floor is filled with doctors and their spouses of all nations and of all dance styles, everyone a little high from the wine and the fellowship and the excitement of being away from home. I am explaining to a doctor whose research involves infant sleep patterns why I don't believe in a benign universe, a personal God: To find God, I say, you look for decay. The doctor smiles warmly at me. I realize I am only flirting. I go over to Anna and ask her where she learned to dance. She tells me: "In my hometown we had no movie; we had weddings and funerals and sometimes parties and the Gypsys came and played music and everyone, children and grown-ups, they danced all night." So Gypsy and Jew were partners in more than just disaster.

We are waiting by the elevators. The night has been long, filled with speeches, music and wine. Tomorrow the conference is over. Anna's eyes are still shining and her body is swaying to the band's last song.

"Why didn't you move to Israel?" I ask.

Her face stiffens. "That was a betrayal on our part," she said. "I feel it all the time. I feel it as a great guilt, the fact that we have chosen our careers in America over living in Israel. A threat to that country can make me disorganized, can give me depression; only a threat to my children's health or happiness can affect me equally."

Standing with Anna at the elevator I feel helpless anger with those who would have destroyed her and again ashamed for having permitted months to go by in which I floated and retreated, for having slept badly over insignificant matters and eaten too much and trembled at shadows and imaginings.

Every wasted second is a kind of betrayal of those who died in the camps, and I have wasted more than my fair share. The elevator comes at last. We say good night, we say good-bye. In a few weeks she is giving a paper on the concept of self at the psychoanalytic meetings in San Francisco. As the elevator doors close I find myself wishing I had given birth to far more Jewish children—communal replacements for Anna's brothers —for others. I remember that Rabbi Greenberg told me that in the DP camps after the war there occurred the highest birthrate of any area in the world. Each birth was a Jewish victory.

Albert Einstein, *Mein Weltbild* (Amsterdam: Querido Verlag, 1934):

"The greatest enemies of the natural conscience and honor of the Jews are fatty degeneration, by which I mean the unconscionableness which comes from wealth and ease . . . and a kind of inner dependence on the surrounding Gentile world which has grown out of the loosening of the fabric of Jewish society. The best in man can only flourish when he loses himself in a community. Hence the moral danger of the Jew who has lost touch with his own people and is regarded as a foreigner by the people of his adoption."

I know what he means. I recognize the emotional sickliness of those who are mounting the assimilation elevator—the pariah worries that he or she may still be a pariah, a parvenu, but without the supports and comforts of a community that bind him to past and future, and he cannot have the illusion that martyrdom is a kind of "happy ending"—a fulfillment of God's wish for His Chosen People.

Albert Einstein goes on to say: "The pursuit of knowledge for its own sake, an almost fanatical love of justice and the desire for personal independence—these are the features of the Jewish tradition that make me thank my stars that I belong to it."

Even if these are the words of Albert Einstein, there is something simplistic about them and they come from clouds of political rhetoric rather than the clear skies of logic. The humanity of Jews lies in their absolute right to be no more perfect, better-mannered, compassionate and justice-loving than anyone else. All peoples' traditions respect goodness and virtue: The Jesuits have learning and the Irish have lust for personal freedom, and the high tone in which most people speak of all these activities is the prerogative of adolescents everywhere.

There are certain ironies in Einstein's statement. The Jews of the ghetto, the Jews of the Middle Ages, the Jews of the great Jewish learning and study, valued not personal freedom but group allegiance and related all activities to their past. Jewish learning in the cheder fosters group agreement, repetition, rather than innovation, and with such strict regulations of behavior, such attention to ritualistic details, that the individual tends to merge with the group, not just in his costume but in his thought as well. It is in the leaving of the group, the adoption of the strangers' ways, that the Jewish mind begins to take on the qualities Einstein spoke of: Freud, Marx, Einstein himself, Kafka, Woody Allen, Charlie Chaplin (Hannah Arendt insists he is Jewish), the molecular physicists Oppenheimer, Niels Bohr, et al. These were all people whose Jewishness was in transition, who were less Jewish than their parents, more exposed to the Gentile world. It is the Jew in transition toward assimilation, plagued by a sense of being outside everybody's world including the Jewish one of his childhood, who has created the image of the modern man with his freedom-loving pursuit of knowledge. It is paradoxical that leaving the Jewish world or partially leaving it creates (like the chemical elements in the sea) the proper conditions for certain kinds of life-forms to emerge. Rabbi Greenberg points out that if the Jews had not been partially Hellenized, the Maccabees would have been unable to fight their enemies on the Sabbath and would have all been slaughtered like their more fundamentalist compatriots.

This is, of course, not to say that learning and studying and building pyramids of mental activities with words have not been the center of the Jewish act of faith since the destruction of the Second Temple, and that David and Saul and the other guerrilla fighters did not long ago establish traditions of nationalism and heroism. All countries have contributed to the total learning of the world and Jews do not have a particularly high percentage of secular scholars, secular critics, creators or lovers of freedom until we begin to see the assimilating Jew—the Jew in tension, out of community, antagonistic and with his hands opening the resistant doors of the Gentile culture. Then the numbers of Jewish seekers of justice, searchers for truth, designers of new utopias, become astounding. In a culture where there may always be rising anti-Semitism, where the Jew may at any time be demeaned and his essence attacked as foreign and evil, it becomes particularly important to declare the Jewish virtues (and that's what Einstein was doing in 1934), even if it is like calling the moon over New York City the most beautiful moon in the world and the sun in Central Park the most extraordinary of suns.

———

I have come up to Riverdale in the Bronx to a neat red-brick house to talk with Rabbi and Blu Greenberg's children. On the walls are Jewish themes in drawings, lithographs and watercolors. On the bookshelves are Jewish history books, Jewish sociology and contemporary works on Israel and Holocaust studies. I have never before met and talked with any Orthodox young people. I do know some adolescents—testy, struggling —with psyches that seem to have been covered with rashes, infected areas and inflamed swellings. At the Greenbergs' dinner table Rabbi Irving Greenberg reads aloud the latest letters from their oldest son, Moshe, who is spending the year at a yeshiva in Israel. The letters are long, affectionate, about studies, people the family knows who have visited in Israel. Moshe has also written a letter to his grandparents. Irving reads that letter also. After the meal the prayers are said. Deborah, the sixteen-year-old daughter, sits at the table after the others have left, finishing reading her prayer book.

David is the second son, and at seventeen he is on the basketball team at the Ramaz School (a Jewish parochial school in Manhattan). He is, like his father, tall and quiet, a kind of deceiving softness in the lanky, liquid movements. He is reserved and yet poised, even though tonight he suffers from a cold and a cough that are clearly affecting his strength. With the kepah on his head, with his long body stretched out in the small living room, he waits for me to talk. He is cautious and dignified, conscious of being the oldest representative of the family in the room.

"You must really talk to Moshe," all the children say to me at some time during the interview. Deborah, at sixteen, is surprising. She is now plump and adolescently shapeless, so that it takes a few moments of talking with her to see the extraordinary beauty in her face, a special kind of loving, a sweetness in the smile and an alertness, a clearness, in the eyes. She attends an all-girls' Jewish religious school in Riverdale. When she speaks she is articulate, quick and, above all, caring. Each question is considered seriously; she is already gently, quietly, asking herself questions, and the seriousness of the ideas she is talking about blends with the openness and honesty of everything about her. As she talked she became more and more sure of herself, beautiful, sweet and even glorious.

JJ (Jonathan-Joseph), who is fourteen and dark-haired and blue-eyed, and is just now like a gangly puppy whose arms and legs move about at odd angles and in unexpected places, is warm, enthusiastic, eager, ready for the adventure of his life and amazed at the world around him. He plans to be a writer. He has already started a novel but gave it up at the beginning of the school term. He wanted to write a book about what it is like to be a Jewish boy today. He is clearly struggling a bit for his place in the family orbit and he wants everyone's respect. He is not, perhaps, the best scholar in the family, but his rush of emotions that mingle with ideas, his urge to understand and explain what's happening to himself, is appealing and somehow graced. More of a clown than his older brother, more of an entertainer, more pushed by feelings that are less under control, he is the one I suspect most likely to suffer from love and lust and get himself tangled in whatever thickets appear. I try not to love him since that would spoil my reporter's objectivity, and confuse my evening's work. The youngest of the group is Goody, who at twelve is nymphlike, still a child and willing to do a lot of things to get attention, and she just might pick a fight, make a scene, demand her share. She is complicated, her dark blue-gray eyes shine with a certain tenseness and, like her mother, she is wary. She wants very much to be good, to say the right thing to me; she is not really sure of herself enough to speak to strangers yet about values and basic issues, and still there is something strong, feisty, unpusharoundable about her.

———

More about the Jewish passion for justice: Albert Einstein was talking about the Jewish identification with the underdog, with the other weak and despised peoples of the earth. Jews have only to use a little imagination to project themselves into the shoes of the blacks or the minorities or the dissidents of any government imprisoned in dungeons the world over. However, as Jews became prosperous, middle class, exactly like their counterparts of other ethnic origins, now they too may vote Republican, join clubs that are exclusive, picket housing projects that threaten their neighborhoods and schools. Jews, like everyone else, have a gravitational group pull toward banality. Those who are not geniuses or saints tend to cheat on their income tax, betray their spouses, make shady deals, use people of influence to obtain special privileges, show off, deceive, ignore their neighbors' tragedies. As Jews become more affluent, as they drift away from the working class and the oppressed class, it will be increasingly difficult to define what is particularly moral about the Jewish people. As Israel becomes more militaristic, more dependent on American military aid, more of a nation like other nations with systems of attack and defense, power over weaker peoples, the Israelis too appear to lose some of the moral fervor that had been defined as special to the Jews. Hannah Arendt pointed out this potential danger in political nationalistic Zionism in 1937.

Ludwig Lewisohn wrote a remarkable story called "The Romantic." A baron in Carpathia, who is the grandson of a Jewish peddler, lives the life of any other aristocrat of his country. He loves Carpathia and longs to be accepted, to be counted a loyal patriot. A dictator comes to power. The baron goes to England and takes an English wife, but a message is sent to him from the dictator, requesting his help in the affairs of the country. The baron returns to Carpathia and at the border he is arrested for treason, put on trial, reviled and executed, because he is a Jew. The baron dies bravely, a Jew at last. The story ends:

Porsony [the captain of the firing squad] and the priest walked over to the body. They bent above it. He had died instantly. They drew themselves up and exchanged glances.

"A brave man," said the priest, with the bitter lines about his mouth deepening.

The captain nodded. "They die game, these Jews. I've seen it before. Do you know what I think sustains them?"

The priest shook his head.

"Their contempt for us and our religion. That's what it is."

As if to ward off a malign influence, the priest crossed himself.

I interview David, Deborah, JJ and Goody Greenberg, February 1980.

AR: What is your favorite moment in the synagogue?

GOODY: I love the priestly blessing, I love the singing on the High Holidays. The priestly blessing is when people over thirteen years old from priestly tribes go up and sing and bless the synagogue. (We're of priestly descent.)

DAVID: I love the holiday Simhat Torah, the rejoicing for the Torah. In the synagogue we take out all the Torahs and everybody gets a chance to carry the Torah. And we dance and sing and go into the street singing and it's just so happy and beautiful. We're celebrating the anniversary of receiving the Torah from Sinai. It's a really happy mood; it's hard to describe.

DEBORAH: We go into the street in front of the public school opposite the synagogue and they are in classes and they come to the window to watch us.

AR: When you say, "Everybody gets a chance to carry the Torah," do you mean women too?

DAVID: Maybe in the Conservative synagogue, but not in the Orthodox, not in ours.

DEBORAH: My favorite moment isn't in the synagogue at all. It's Friday night when my mother and Goody and I welcome in the Sabbath Queen. There is such a peaceful atmosphere when we sing. Maybe I just like it so much because that is my mother's favorite moment and everything is so quiet and nice.

JJ: We all stand at the end of the prayer and face the door. It's sort of a magic kind of feeling.

DEBORAH: The women light the candles to bring the Sabbath and the peace into the house. My father and brothers are usually at shul but we are almost always home. It's sort of our special time.

JJ: Everything about the Sabbath is terrific, especially the singing at Friday dinner and Saturday lunch. We always argue about which songs to sing and we are always trying to get them to sing fewer and shorter ones, but still the singing is really special on the Shabbas.

AR: What is your most personal religious moment? When have you felt closest to God?

DEBORAH: I know exactly. I know just when. I was eleven years old and I was on my first trip to Israel. We went to the Wall of the Temple in Jerusalem and all around me the women were praying and some of them were crying. I could hear my heart beat. I was overwhelmed with God. I could feel Him there. I wrote a note and put it in the Wall. I wrote in my note that God should protect my family, Abba and Ema, Moshe and David and JJ and Goody and that we should be able to come back to Israel soon. Last summer we were in Israel and I went back to the Wall and saw just where I had put my note but I didn't feel the same thing at all. When I was young I had felt so much. Maybe it's because I was at an impressionable age. I don't know for sure.

JJ: There isn't really one religious moment for me, but I can tell you when I most identify with being Jewish. It's when I go with my school to rallies against the PLO or to help Soviet Jews. Then I identify with God and being Jewish. I feel proud of being a Jew. I look forward to rallying. Even though it's cold or something I feel glad. I think that the Russian Jews could get stuck in Siberia where it's much colder. I think I'm with God and He'll help us. I feel good then.

AR: Are you directing the rally toward God or some political force or powers?

JJ: It's really both. The Russian Jews that are getting out are being helped by God and by us.

DAVID: The Wall was also a strong thing for me too. I see myself in a composite of small religious experiences, not just one big one.

GOODY: When I'm doing something Jewish and I'm surrounded by my friends, then I feel most Jewish.

DEBORAH: My parents are thinking of moving us to live in Israel in a few years. We have a lot of family and friends there as well as here.

GOODY: I know that I'm going someday to settle in Israel but I think I'd like to start and get my education here in America.

AR: What do you want to learn?

GOODY (laughs, looks away and giggles): I haven't told anybody yet. I don't want them to tease me.

DAVID: It's all right, Goody. Just say it. We won't laugh.

GOODY (in a very low voice): Maybe computer science.

JJ: You can do that in Israel. They have computers in Israel.

GOODY: I suppose.

The news is all about Cubans. Cubans in Miami rushing off in little boats to rescue other Cubans from Fidel's paradise. The Cubans have their own terrorists. They have their heroes and antiheroes and they too stay together. Five hundred thousand Cuban exiles have raised enough money to give forty dollars to every new refugee setting foot on United States soil. It reminds me of the organizations, the Alliance and settlement houses that provided the initial feeding and help for the Jewish refugees who were coming by the hundred thousands after 1900. The Cubans are reacting to this present crisis as if they were Jews.

Is group loyalty an automatic by-product of any oppression? If the boatloads of Cubans were Jews, would they have been turned back in the high seas as the boats of Nazi victims were? I am wondering if one feels a primary identification with all the boat peoples afloat on all the waters of the globe, can there ever be a return to the particular group again? Can one switch easily back and forth from a universal to a singular view? Passion for justice seems to weaken in us as the cluster we identify with grows larger and less specific. If one is not involved in a specific cause or unit, eventually the capacity for empathy disappears (like blowing up a balloon too far until it bursts).

"The assimilated Jew," one nineteenth-century philosopher said, "was the idolator of his own ego."

The Greenberg children interview continued:

AR: What do the rest of you want to do with your lives?
DEBORAH: I'm thinking of fashion or photography or something like that. This summer I'm going to work in my father's organization [The National Jewish Resource Center]. Maybe I'd like to do that kind of work when I grow up.
JJ: I want to write books. I want to tell more than just my friends and family what I feel about being a Jew and all. I want to write about everything that happens to me and how that related to Judaism, to living as a Jew.
AR: Do you feel different, special, being Jewish, when you go to school, when you move around in America, in New York; what do you feel?

DAVID: I know I'm different. I consider myself religious, so I am different. I don't necessarily look different except for my kepah, but I know I'm different inside.

DEBORAH: I find it hard to identify myself as a Jew around other people. I don't wear a star or a letter or anything. I'm not able to wear a kepah because I'm a girl. Maybe I should wear a star, but once in school one of the girls asked the rabbi how to show people she was Jewish. He said she should take out her chain with the letter on it and wave it in people's faces. But I don't know, I just can't do that. Maybe I should. But when I'm in a bus I always get up and give an older person my seat.

JJ: We all do that because we're Jews, because we were brought up good.

DEBORAH: I find it hard to show, about being Jewish. I feel people are always watching me, whether it's to catch me or what?

AR: To catch you? At what?

DEBORAH: I guess because I'm different that they'll resent it or be intrigued by me or there'll be some kind of anti-Semitism or maybe they are just curious.

JJ: I always strongly identify myself with being Jewish. I started this fad of wearing big fuzzy socks and lots of big odd shirts, clothes that were out of the ordinary. I always wear my yarmulke on my head. I always wonder what people are looking at when they stare at me, whether it's my socks, my clothes, my chipped front teeth (I did it years ago playing ball). I figure people specially stare at my yarmulke. But they are especially surprised by all of me. (*He grins ear to ear, showing very chipped teeth.*)

AR: Do you think Jews are smarter than everyone else?

GOODY: Sometimes it does seem to me that the rabbis are teaching us that we are superior, but I don't know. Maybe it's just that after all we are the Chosen People and so we have a closer relationship with God. I don't feel that we're smarter, I think we're special.

DAVID: You can't really say that all Jews are smart. There are brilliant scientists who are Jewish and some who are not. But I really believe that to a larger extent, higher education is more honored in the Jewish structure, and education more deeply rooted in the family beliefs. An unusually high percentage of Nobel Prize winners have been Jewish.

A cousin whose life has taken an uncertain turn has begun a hunt for the family roots. An announcement has come in the mail that on May 29 there will be a formal unveiling at the Yivo Institute for Jewish Research of the family history and all members of the family are invited to come to this historic presentation. In America in 1980 it seemed unlikely that a full chart of all the family names, marriages and divorces, offspring and offspring's offspring would serve to reattach the split and dried wood of the family tree. We could not, merely by learning the names and dates, restore ourselves to the full vigor, the moment of immigrant grit and guts that made my grandfather who barely went to school see his conditions in life undergo such a radical and materially positive change. My brother, always the scientist, has suggested that what we really need is a list of all the illnesses and causes of death in the family, a counting up of manic-depressives (this is a common illness among some Ashkenazi and we have had our share), a counting of heart deaths and cancer deaths and the ages of those. At least, my brother says, "those statistics might give us something to think about. The names and dates, who cares? What will that explain?" Even Gluckel knew that if you wanted to leave a record for your children you had to flesh it out with details of the quality of life: the way you loved, the way people did things, the way they lost, and include the things that both embarrassed as well as those that gratified. A doctored, retouched family history won't soothe old wounds.

We go to see a movie about union organizing in a textile mill in the South. Norma Rae is the proud Southern heroine and a Jewish labor man from New York named Reuben is the hero. What makes you a Jew? asks Norma Rae. "History," answers Reuben, and the New York audience laughs. I am uncomfortable. My father's major client was the family shirt company. My governess who taught me how to eat with a spoon, my education, my party dress and the winter coats, my dancing lessons, my doctor bills, my childhood food and shelter were all well paid for by the dividends from the shirt company. My mother had inherited stock at thirteen when her father had died. (Hero-of-the-pushcart, he died too early and left his children too well off.) I am management. I can pretend it all had nothing to do with me. In fact, I can say I have never read an annual report all the way through or attended a stockholders' meeting. I can say I was a Marxist before I was old enough to know history, and afterward a liberal, a Leftist, a woman of the people with the people, but finally I must own to the hypocrisy. I see certain unwelcome contradictions. I am a person whose morality was paid for by the hard labor of people who were probably not earning enough, in conditions that were suffocating. I am the product of the wits of my grandfather. I am the freethinker whose free thoughts were paid for by others with less free thoughts. In the movie the bosses are flat-faced and implacable, the working people are real, tired and abused. In the movie theater I lean close to my husband. He rests his cheek against mine. A woman in the row behind me taps me on the shoulder.

"When you lean together like that I can't see." She's angry. After all, she paid for a ticket.

We pull apart. I don't want to be responsible for blocking out her vision.

Greenberg children interview continued:

DAVID: Jews have more opportunity to show off their smarts and refine their minds.

AR: What are the Chosen People chosen for? For what?

DEBORAH: I'm not sure I understand the concept of being chosen. Lots of Jews use that idea to feel better than other people. I don't believe that's true.

When I was eleven years old the War of Independence in Israel was beginning. Camps in Cyprus were overflowing with survivors. The Swedish Count Bernadotte (a United Nations mediator) was assassinated. Even my father, who had never before been involved in his Jewishness, made Zionist speeches at the dinner table. Boats outside the three-mile limit were dropping refugees into the water and Jewish swimmers were ferrying the war-exhausted passengers to the shores. One summer near my parents' house, some swimmers were in training. For a while there was color, adventure and purpose in our lives. My parents gave several parties to raise money for guns and equipment to be smuggled into the forces of the Haganah or the Irgun. In Sunday school, we gave our allowances for trees to be planted in Eretz Israel.

An army man, a former British army captain, now part of the underground in Palestine, came to New York and spoke at fund-raising parties. He wore his fatigues, his beret, and he was leathery and had a black mustache. I thought he was a knight, a hero beyond compare. I thought the death he seemed willing to accept for the statehood, the redemption of his people, of remarkable beauty. He may have been my first love. He smelled of altruism, pride and morality. He gave me hope that there was after all some value and purpose in my growing up. I might not have to be a woman whose breakfast was brought to her in bed; the world was wider than I had known. I was a romantic, he was an army man. Unfortunately, he had a daughter my age who was interested in ballet and was a trifle stupid. At the fund-raising meetings I, in a velvet dress and Mary Janes, passed around the checkbook and collected the offerings. I wanted to do more . . . but more was not asked.

Post-1948 my army hero got a public relations job with an airline and came to New York to settle and joined my father's athletic club. So much for my early taste in men.

The hope of Israel, the hardness of life, the pioneer energy it would require, all those opened escape hatches. When I was sixteen and no longer religious or very Jewish, I daydreamed that perhaps I would meet a traveling Israeli soldier who would marry me and take me back to his kibbutz. I imagined him with his strong back sweating in the hot sun, planting orange trees while I rode a tractor over the green fields that had shortly before been desert.

Question: Why did I not dream of going to Israel myself? After all, lots of young women did, including, at an early time, Golda Meir herself. Youth groups existed, there were ways to go, travel groups and schools offering programs. The fact was that I followed the crowd, imagined only the reality of my parents' life, did as was expected and had neither the strength nor the independence to break across the sea into a new place. I had not the courage of my grandparents who had traveled a wide sea for a new home. I saw the need to jump but I could not send the right messages to the muscles. I froze. My search became internal and the small steps I took were only psychological. I shuffled into adulthood, head down against the wind. I needed a Prince Charming to wake me from my sleep. I thought I was only a shadow that would be given life by the perfect kiss. I was afraid to go from the things I knew, even if those things could not sustain me. That is an old familiar story by now; I was not the only American female in that predicament and we have all heard enough of that.

And then new interests took over, other less dramatic paths of escape appeared. Books and modern dance, Broadway theater, the wonderful weary bohemianism of the fifties that required a cynicism, a posture of despair, that did not fit with the Sabra that might have been, Thomas Mann, Proust, Picasso, Tolstoy, André Gide, Thoreau, Emerson, Henry James. The education I was receiving was making me more and more a universal citizen and less and less a Jew. I had now multiple loyalties. What kind of existentialist wearing black leotard and sandals can also be a Zionist? In mood, if nothing else, those were contradictory positions.

Do I look back now and wish I had gone to Israel? Yes, but I would also have liked to have been a concert pianist, an abstract painter, a field hockey player, a mountain climber, a rancher in Colorado, a social worker among the Indians of New Mexico, a pediatrician in Harlem. What is memory but a catalog of opportunities missed?

Rabbi Kasriel Kastel (wearing black beard, black coat and yarmulke) of the Lubavitcher Chasidic movement speaks to a roomful of Jewish writers, publishers, lawyers, historians, and so forth, who meet informally once a month in an apartment on Central Park West to discuss the meaning of their Jewishness, to explore their mutual involvement over who they are and where they came from. Rabbi Kastel is in the business of Tshouvot (returning): He is a missionary with a cause, our souls. He is indirect, informative; he is used to talking to the likes of this crowd.

Rabbi Kastel says that it is foolish to question God about the Holocaust or any other evil. He describes a primitive man

from the deepest bush coming for the first time into a modern
hospital and looking in the operating room. Here he would see
men chopping open another man, machines, blood, steel
knives. It would look to this primitive like a ritual slaughter,
like a cruelty beyond cruelties. How else could he interpret
what he sees? So we too are like the creatures of the primeval
forest and must accept God's direction and will and assume
His purposes that are beyond our understanding are benign.
The image is vivid, appealing. For a split second I wonder if
I could accept that. I veer toward faith and then I pull back.
I think of the simplistic and childish nature of that explanation. God has provided no anesthetic in His operating room,
unless we assume that religion itself is the anesthetic, and I
cannot accept God as the Good-Surgeon-in-the-Sky. Whatever
tumors He may be removing, He has also planted there.

Rabbi Kastel explains about the proselytizing work of his
group. He describes the mitzvah mobile that tries to reintro-
duce Jewish males to the ritual of laying on t'fillin. He feels
that the Torah was given on Sinai to Moses and that the Jews
should live as they have always lived: What was right for the
grandfathers is also right for the grandsons. He fields all questions about women's position with descriptions of the importance of the women's role in the Jewish home. He talks about
the wonderful uses of modern technology the Lubavitcher have
made: phone connections to synagogues around the world,
organizing techniques for children's marches that would make
any media expert envious. He does not describe the one-way
mirror in the synagogue that permits the women in the balcony
to look down but prevents the men from seeing and being
tempted by the women. Ah, technology!

Rabbi Kastel describes the belief of the Cabala—a belief he
shares—that all the souls who had left Egypt with Moses and
crossed the divided sea are still with us today in different
bodies. He believes that all souls move through many different
bodies and in the final End of Days when the Messiah comes
and the dead are risen there will be (as the sun can shine in

many windows) soul enough for all the bodies to come to life again eternally. For the Chasidim, God keeps the world alive as the soul keeps the body alive; each soul is an extension of God.

Rabbi Kastel talks about the founder of his movement, the great and famous Baal Shem Tov, a teacher of the ignorant rural Jaws who were despised by both the Gentiles and their more learned city Jewish relatives. The Baal Shem Tov brought joy and dance and intimacy into the worship of God. He began the equivalent of the Baptist Church in comparison to the Catholic. He opened the religion for the ignorant and made all male Jews equally "holy." He found a route to God that did not require years of study and a gift for academic learning, but he made of himself and his leader successors heroes, men larger than life whose every word was to be followed. He brought equality between the learned and the ignorant while imposing a new kind of subjection to a new authority!

Rabbi Kastel tells of the great emotional conflict in his community during the last celebration of Simhat Torah (when Jews must be happy) because their rabbi had a heart attack. The rabbi commanded them to go on experiencing the joy of the holiday despite their concern for him. They continued to celebrate because he wished it. The enormous authority of the rabbi comes clear as Rabbi Kastel speaks with love and reverence of the great leaders of the Lubavitcher in the past and present. If the rabbi wants someone to continue his studies in the outside world, then it is permitted. If the rabbi wants a man to give up his interest in medicine or whatever, the interest is abandoned. As Rabbi Kastel talks he describes a world in which the individual has given up areas of autonomy for which we in Western society have fought hard and long. The world of the religious person can so easily become theocratic. The authority that binds the group together consumes the self and a trade is made.

Rabbi Kastel, sitting on a couch near a table set with wine

and cheese, describes the dilemma facing the Russian Jews as Napoleon made his amazing march across the map of Europe. The Russian Jews could at first not decide whether to support the czar or to support Napoleon. Napoleon offered emancipation of the Jews. He was breaking down ghetto walls and repealing the laws of discrimination and exclusion that had confined the Jews everywhere before the French Revolution. He was eliminating the isolation that kept the Jewish communities impoverished and cut off from the rest of modern Europe. After some debate the Chasidim decided to support the czar because they were afraid that emancipation would fragment and destroy their religion. (You have to be very clever to step on your own toes to save wear on your feet.)

One of the Chasidim became a spy for the czar while serving on Napoleon's inner council. The Chasidim believe that mind controls emotion, that rationality leads feelings wherever it wants. The autumn just before the fatal snows and the long winter that forced Napoleon to retreat, Napoleon announced to his council that there was a spy among them and that he was going to hold his hand over the heart of each of them and say that the person he was touching was the spy and the guilty person would be unable to prevent his heart from beating faster and Napoleon would recognize his enemy. The Chasid, because of his fine religious training, was able to control his heartbeat and so deceived the first lie-detector test ever invented. Oh, psychosomatic medicine, oh, mind-over-body arguments. The disciplines of God give great power over the body but they didn't save these same Chasidim from the rampages and the pogroms of the czar they had so loyally defended. Oh, poor Napoleon, whose crime may have been not to have been anti-Semitic enough!

Gluckel, of course, would have been right at home in the Lubavitcher community in Brooklyn, even though the year is 1980 and Gluckel herself barely had a toe in the eighteenth century. On the other hand, a reincarnated Gluckel might have very quickly moved into the world of general commerce and owned Bergdorf Goodman by now and sent her sons to Harvard and her daughters to Yale. . . . Who knows?

Rabbi Kastel says that before the Lubavitcher rabbi came to America in the 1940s and started his yeshiva, America was a godless place. He says that on the ocean floor rises a huge mountain of t'fillin thrown overboard by generations of migrating Jews, fleeing the cheders of their youth and looking to the New World, to Americanization, to assimilation.

"An ocean full of t'fillin," repeats Rabbi Kastel.

"I can see why," whispers one of the members of the audience.

———

I am attending our block association meeting in New York City. We discuss our annual auction and raffle, our planting of ivy around the trees, and we form a food committee for our spring party and adjourn for drinks. In the kitchen of my neighbor's house one of my new neighbors, in the loud, nasal boom of the society matron, announces that she is a devout Episcopalian but was shocked to discover on joining the Church of the Heavenly Rest that the minister had just divorced his wife to marry the widow of a prominent member of the congregation.

"Marriage of ministers should be stable," she pronounced. "What kind of an example is that?"

"Well," said another of my neighbors (who has pointed out to me so often that his children are blond and blue-eyed and Aryan-looking that I begin to suspect a black grandmother in the closet, or maybe just a Jewish one), "I am an atheist but we are sending our children to the Church of the Heavenly Rest Sunday school, and we have joined because I want them to know who they are and not just from some half-assed college religion course. I want them to know their Bible history."

Assimilation, then, which implies the breaking down of the

old ties, a thinning of connections, is also a Christian problem. My neighbor, who has tried swinging-couples groups, transactional analysis, physical fitness and liberal politics, is as confused as the rest of us. But unlike Jews, as he and his wife try out new life-styles that might cause their parents heart palpitations, they do not move drastically from one time period to another, they do not cross languages, and learn new sets of manners and cement new hopes onto old forms. Their assimilation problems require less dislocation and release fewer electric charges into the atmosphere. They can smoke pot in their backyard, go to a different church each Sunday, without burning too many bridges.

It may be the effect of working on this book for many months now, it may be the result of constant reading of Jewish history, but I am feeling a new and peculiar irrational hostility to my Christian neighbors. I have images of blood ritual accusations, little massacres, burnings, expulsions from large countries and small fiefdoms, rapes, stonings, autos-da-fé, and of course the Holocaust. My head is bulging with memories of hatred violently acted out and continual, constant like the spring rains and the winter snow. I hold my drink in my hand in my neighbor's living room and I remember the report from the Warsaw ghetto of a German (raised in Christian Sunday schools), a young soldier of the SS who, after being told the purpose of the medicine phials, smashed to bits the remaining insulin supply of a diabetic Jewish child. I cannot think about Christian charity and goodness. I am not impressed with the moral tradition my neighbors' children will learn in that Sunday school of the Church of the Heavenly Rest. The Gospel according to Matthew, Mark, Luke and John works as well as reciting the story of the little pigs to Jack the Ripper as he is about to go out into the London night. Of course I walk to the window and attempt to restore my sense of proportion. I take a deep breath. To read history is to dislike whoever is in charge, whoever the upper classes, the majority in power, may be. Of course it was not Christianity that caused the

Inquisition but the all too human misuse of it. But a great religion must take responsibility for its failure to civilize its followers. A great religion that cannot subdue the human need to destroy and attack is simply not great, not good enough. The more I read of Jewish history the less friendly to the outside world I feel, the more there becomes an inner and outer world, a Jewish and non-Jewish world. But if I start to hate this Episcopalian neighbor for crimes she never committed, I will turn myself into the very kind of monster I am most afraid of. If I stop looking at her as a particular woman with name and face and anxieties just like mine, then I transform myself into the beast. On the other hand, how to avoid the clear recognition that her class, her religion, have left unmet certain crucial responsibilities? Does she as an individual hold any responsibility for that?

A rabbi and his wife also live on our block. I have never spoken to him because he looks so stern and forbidding. Tonight I walk over to talk to the rabbi's wife. She wears a thick black wig and her accent sounds German, though I'm not certain. She's a heavy woman whose legs seem bowed under the weight of her torso. She is clearly a woman who has never run around the Central Park reservoir or held a tennis racket or taken a prize in a horse show. We talk. The rabbi's wife is concerned because my daughter, I tell her, had swallowed a button earlier in the day.

"You must get a strainer and watch carefully her stool," she tells me. "My twin girls," she adds, "when they were little they swallowed things too." She smiles at me and her dark eyes look into mine with protectiveness as if we were not strangers at all. I feel oddly shy. I feel oddly in need of mothering myself. Could she be like Gluckel? Has she read Gluckel? I want to ask her but I am shy.

My great-uncle Max, one of my grandfather's younger brothers, was (according to my mother) not much of a businessman. As the shirt business grew and grew they found him increasingly more bother than help. Eventually they gave him a lot of stock, some honorary title and happily he went to New Jersey and bought himself a little estate. He developed a passion for polo, which quite shocked the family. He taught himself how to play. He bought some horses and he applied to the local polo club for membership. They had never had an application from a Jew before (especially a little bald Jew with an accent). They turned him down flat. He wasn't discouraged. He hired two teams to come play polo with him twice a month. Everyone in the family laughed at him. He drank too much and went off to the Happy Polo Grounds in the Sky. He was, probably the first Jew from the Lower East Side, whose Yiddish was not yet dead in his mouth, to play polo.

———

I am beginning my freshman year at Smith College. The year is 1953, a bland year in crops of women. The generation is, so they say, apathetic, conforming and docile. The girls are wearing Bermuda shorts and gold circle pins. The sophomores and juniors sport a fraternity pin on their shirt collars. They are announcing in Ivy League code that they are engaged to be engaged to a boy from Dartmouth, Harvard, Yale or Princeton. The campus is covered with maples turning red and yellow. Girls on bikes are pedaling up the hills toward the library or to classes in red-brick buildings whose architecture, Georgian, Victorian, promises prosperity and dignity forever after. I am assigned to a dormitory and on my floor and in my half of the floor are a group of Jewish girls from New York and Shaker Heights, Ohio. I have noticed and am annoyed. I am assigned a big sister to help me through the confusing first weeks away from home. She is a Jewish girl from Brooklyn. She wants me immediately to join the Hillel Society (the Jewish organization on campus). I hedge. I dodge. I postpone. I do a little questioning. The Catholic girls have Catholic big sisters and join the Newman Club. The Protestant girls have Protestant big sisters and don't have to join anything. In several places, the dormitory rooms for freshmen have been assigned according to religion. I am outraged. This is America. This is supposed to be a melting pot. I am seventeen and can recognize an injustice even if it is hiding under the bed. I am too innocent to realize that our dormitory arrangements are preparation for real life when we will all go off to our respective suburbs and join our respective country clubs and religious organizations and ultimately be buried in the cemetery of our denomination. I am furious. I believe in the brotherhood of man and the ideal of the melting pot. I am not afraid of homogenization because I have not yet experienced it. I will not join the Hillel Society. I consider myself free to mingle with whomever I choose. This involves some isolation till I find the other misfits on the campus. Finally I befriend one painter, one poet, one art historian; only by coincidence are they all Jewish.

I find a boy from Amherst. His name is Roger. He is not Jewish. He has an athletic scholarship and is on the swimming team because of his terrific butterfly crawl. He is angular, pale and very nervous. He writes me long poems about snails crawling around the rims of glasses. He comes to pick me up and announces his name at the front desk. My big sister comes into my room as I am deciding which pair of Bermuda shorts to wear for the evening.

"You shouldn't go out with non-Jewish boys. We don't think that's such a good idea." She adds, "Don't you realize your traditions are important to you? We don't want to see you make a terrible mistake."

I feel claustrophobic. I open the window wide. I stick my head out. I breathe deep gulps of the blue New England air.

I am an American, I claim. I will not be cornered into one place. This is the land of liberty. I am climbing out of the ghetto; even the gilded ghetto is no place for me. I am standing on the rooftops, I am gone.

"Thank you for your advice," I say to my big sister. "I appreciate it. I will think about it."

Roger sends me more poetry that I don't understand. Is it brilliant or just incoherent? We neck in front of the dormitory at curfew hour. He tells me dark secrets that make me sad. His demons are alarming. I am enjoying being alarmed. Just before Thanksgiving vacation his roommate calls me. Roger is in the infirmary. He has had a nervous breakdown. He is going home to Louisville to be hospitalized. I am not surprised. Everybody interesting is crazed. I am at an age when neither mental balance nor safety seems sexy.

"Let me introduce you," says my big sister, "to some Jewish boys."

"No, thank you," I say. I spend months in the doughnut shop eating till I am temporarily out of shape, benched, so to speak, from the game.

I call Rabbi Alan Miller of the Society for the Advancement of Judaism.

"Are you the lady who wrote the article on having a Christmas tree a year ago?" he asks.

"I am."

"Well," he says, "I don't appreciate you. I don't want to talk to you."

Rabbi Miller is referring to an article I wrote for *The New York Times* that described our family Christmas and my ambivalence about having a tree and a Christmas celebration in our house. The article was a brief observation of life on the assimilated plane. I described my uneasiness when the neighborhood rabbi saw us carry in our tree, and I talked about the way we as a family enjoyed the very secular Christmas we celebrated. I talked about being unable, as a nonreligious Jew, to create a Channukah holiday in our house. So dim was my memory of Sunday-school lessons that in the article I even mixed up the Syrians and the Roman invaders of Palestine in a brief allusion. Many Jews, some of them dear friends, were angry and upset that I had published this article. Many readers were enraged that I would push my views of religion or ceremony or affiliation on others. I had not meant to prescribe but to describe, but this subject of assimilation is so rooted in fears and animosities that merely bringing up the matter became for some readers an incendiary, provocative act. I had thought that I was writing a slight life-style piece and was surprised at the angry response from strangers, the threats and curses we received by mail or phone. I had obviously broken a taboo, crossed into a forbidden space. Writers of course are always drawn to just such places.

I am sorry that Rabbi Miller doesn't want to talk with me but as I hang up the phone (feeling hurt by his stiffness and his angry voice), I realize that I don't want to talk to him either. His hostility will evoke my defensiveness and if I write or think with the goal of defending myself I will do violence both to the honesty of my original questions and the possibilities of meaningful answers. I must also remember that for many people the questions I have are already settled are not open to re-examination. These people will not understand or appreciate my grapplings. Since I am unable to talk to Rabbi Miller I will advance, delay, retrogress or circle around my Judaism without him. Blu Greenberg said that when she had read the article in The New York Times she had not been angry but instead had felt sorry for me that I had not been given the Jewish home life that would have made it possible for me to distinguish emotionally between a Christmas tree and a Channukah menorah. She felt sorry that I had been deprived of the things that came to her as part of her natural birthright. It made me angry to have her "feel sorry." Pity is a particularly nasty intellectual weapon.

Tomorrow is my daughter Becky's tenth birthday. We are having a costume party. She has planned to be a gnome. I am making a cake and have spent two good days on the planning, on the favors, on the decorations. My husband is bemused, although by now resigned. When he was a child in Brooklyn he had no birthday parties because no one in that neighborhood had heard of the tradition. It's an American custom, not from the old country, not in the Jewish ghettos of Russia and Poland. His mother and father, who had arrived here in their late teens, did not think of making their American-born son a birthday party with hats and candy and friends to help blow out the candles on the cake.

I have a picture of myself at a birthday party. I am perhaps three or four. I am watching a magician with a group of other children. My governess stands in the doorway with the other governesses. They are all wearing white uniforms. They are smiling at the magician. I am in velvet and party shoes and my hair has been brushed as straight as possible. I look at the other governesses: Shinke, Ilse, Greta and Hanna. Guardians of my childhood companions. All the governesses are German and all the children are Jewish and the year is 1938. In the picture I see my friends Harry Moses, Michael Mazur and Nancy Schwartz. We are all very clean in all our personal parts. We are all very plump, soft, flabby children who wet their beds, who suck their thumbs and are afraid forever of dark closets and loud noises.

Now I am filling the party bags for Becky's birthday. I also insist on fresh flowers and balloons. The birthday of each of the children has become a ritual holiday. It marks a year's passage and it reaffirms the child's welcome in the world. The birthday is the holiday of individual glory. It is the child's momentary place at the center of things. "The cake is for me." "The presents are for me." "I am the cause and the subject of the celebration." Even as I place the candles in the frosting I am having reservations. Is this the holiday of narcissists? Is this the way to create a society of Self and Me? Do we as a culture celebrate ego instead of community? Is this festival (American-learned, new in our family history) teaching the "idolatry of the self"?

Oh, well, perhaps I am being too heavy about it all. Sociology in the hands of amateurs can turn to lead. The birthday is after all such a brief moment of grandiosity. A bare second in the center of the universe does not mean one will insist on staying there and we must have some ritual, some celebration, in this house. We have no harvest festival, no spring dance. We have so few occasions to mark rite and passage and to pause to experience the pleasure of our everydayness. I tie the balloons to the chandelier. After the party my husband and I will open a bottle of wine. We will toast Becky. We will be thankful for the wholeness of her body and the uniqueness of her soul. We will feel tender toward each other because we created her together. Our pleasure will not be without the knowledge that we are also afraid of illness, accident, of other tragedies that hover in the shadows, waiting their turn to come forward and reveal themselves.

I am twelve years old at a girls' camp in Maine. I love camp. I love field hockey, tennis and baseball. I love the tall pines and the canoes and the ice-cold morning air and the oil lamps that glow at night under the stars on the bunkhouse steps. I love the counselors, who are tall and athletic, who go to physical education schools in Boston and don't ever wear makeup or high heels. They smell clean and honest. They talk about sportsmanship and integrity and trying harder and doing your best. They talk about independence in the woods and survival in the water. They don't talk about money or men. I would give anything in the world for them to approve of me. I make plans to grow up and become a gym teacher too. I love archery, hiking and learning the names of the birds and the trees. My fellow campers are all Jewish children from prosperous suburbs and the older established Jewish enclaves in Atlanta, Nashville and Cleveland. There are many from Elkins Park, Pennsylvania, Scarsdale and Great Neck, New York. The counselors are all Methodists, Presbyterians, Yankees. The owners of the camp are two older German Jewish women named Aunt Caroline and Miss Kitty.

One morning the whole camp is summoned to a meeting after the raising of the flag on the flagpole that stands inside the circle of tents around which the bugle plays at the appropriate hours. We are all looking forward to overnight camping trips to the mountains and lakes of Maine. We will be driven by bus to starting points on the Rangeley Lakes and to the base of Mount Washington. At this meeting we are told what to pack and who is going in which group. Then Aunt Caroline asked all the counselors to please leave the meeting. This was an unusual procedure. When the last of them had gone into their bunks or up to the main house, she told us that Jewish people tended to be very loud and aggressively noisy and that the people of Maine would hear us and make remarks about Jews and so we should try to be very quiet and dignified when going through towns or stopping in public places where natives might hear us.

"You must not give them reason to dislike you. You must control your loud Jewish voices."

There was silence among the campers. The meeting was dismissed. I went back to my bunk and wrote and asked my mother to come and get me and take me home. I went to Aunt Caroline and Miss Kitty and told them that those remarks were prejudiced. Jews were not louder than anyone else,

I said. Aunt Caroline pointed out that I was the only camper who did not see complete justice in her words. She said I was too young to understand that there were real ethnic differences among people, and that Jews did indeed tend to be loud and emotional and noisy. I tried to explain my point of view to my friends and counselors. No one seemed to understand why I was so upset. Everyone tried to jolly me out of my bad mood. A few days later we went out of camp on our trips. Whenever I saw Maine people in candy stores by the side of roads or on the lake, I yelled and screamed my loudest. I felt I owed that noise to someone.

Greenberg children interview continued:

AR: How do you reconcile the idea of God with the Holocaust?
JJ: In the novel *Night* by Elie Wiesel, the boy suffers not only from hunger and everything, but because he thinks God has abandoned him. When Moses asks God at the burning bush, "What is your name?" God says, "I will be what I will be." But in another commentary, God says when the Jewish people need Me I will be there and in the Holocaust He was not there. I have some difficulty understanding that, some conflict about that. It's really impossible to find the right answer.
DEBORAH: About the Holocaust, nobody will be able to justify or deny it, but I know something, that for the rest of my life it's going to be one thing I'm going to keep from happening again.
DAVID: I don't think that the Jews who were in the Holocaust had sinned. I think the idea that people would be punished like that has to be dispelled. I dismiss that right away. I think there are many answers but I don't know what is true. Suffering is always a paradox (*laughs shyly*). This gets right

into my father's thinking. It really gives me trouble. I sometimes don't sleep nights thinking about it. I guess it will
continue to haunt me.

AR: What do you think about the Messiah coming?

GOODY: It scares me to think about it. So many Jews will die and
not be resurrected. Am I such a great person that I'm going
to be there, and even if I am, is my family going to be
there with me? That's always frightened me.

I find it hard to understand all the suffering in Jewish
history. The Holocaust is the worst. Who am I to question
God? But sometimes I hear things that make me so mad
and so upset. The Holocaust is the only thing I really have
against God. I'm obsessed to know the answer why, to find
out the truth.

DEBORAH: I have a recurring nightmare that my family is in Nazi
Germany and somehow they let everyone escape except me
and the Nazis chase me through a crack in our garage door
and I think I'm safe but when I look up I see Hitler sitting
in an armchair with Goebbels at his side. The dream is like
Animal Farm, sort of. The soldiers look like pigs and Russians and Nazis at the same time. I wake up in a sweat.

AR: Do you believe that the Messiah will come in your lifetime?

ALL FOUR CHILDREN: Oh, yes! Well, maybe.

JJ: The Messiah could be living now. He doesn't have to be an
angel. It could be that we will have a gradual change to a
perfect world. There are many people my age who might be
the Messiah. It would be very nice if it happened in my
lifetime.

DEBORAH: Some rabbis in Israel thought that the Messiah might
come on my birthday this year. But I don't even know exactly what the Messiah is.

DAVID: I hope that the Messiah will come. I see a lot of things
wrong with society today. I'd be really happy if the Messiah would come. I think it is possible.

DEBORAH: I don't think so really. I don't think it is possible. I
can't predict for sure.

AR: What would happen if the Messiah came?

GOODY: I'm a little afraid. It's part of my faith but it's sort of frightening to think of. I'd be overjoyed, but right now I just don't know.

DEBORAH: I'd always pictured it as if we returned to Biblical times in white robes. We'd all be together again, a regiving of life, a resurrection of all the dead people who were good.

DAVID: We believe in the world to come, not life after death. We learn that if you are good enough you will be part of the world to come. I hope I make it. If you respect your parents you have a chance for the Olam Haban [world to come].

JJ: Everybody will live together in peace in Israel. There will be no more religious differences. Everybody will be the same. Nobody will think they are better than anyone else.

DEBORAH: If we go back to olden times after the Messiah comes, women will have an even worse role than now. That really worries me.

AR: Do you believe there should be women rabbis?

DEBORAH: Yes, definitely. It is not in the Torah that there shouldn't be women; only the rabbis said so.

JJ: In our family in grace after meals we believe that women can say the prayers. Most Jews believe that you need three men over thirteen, but we think it's all right to use women or have the women do it alone.

GOODY: But you won't sit down with us.

JJ: I will. And so will David and Moshe. At first they didn't want to, but now I think they will.

DEBORAH: As our society changes this will change. The rabbis may have misinterpreted or misunderstood.

AR: If you could change something in your religion, what might it be?

DAVID: It is hard to think of myself having the power to change things. I can't imagine it.

DEBORAH: I'd like to stop all the arguing among ultra-Orthodox, Conservative and Reform; one group looks down on the other and there are antagonisms among the groups. It's not constructive. I wish it could stop and we could be united.

JJ: I would permit women to be rabbis and men and women to sit together. I think people would watch themselves more if everyone were equal.

AR: Tell me about the books you especially like or are important to you.

JJ: I liked *Sherlock Holmes* and *Jonathan Livingston Seagull*.

DAVID: I think my favorite book is *Catch-22*. I was reading Simon Wiesenthal's *Wanted*, but halfway through it I felt such a rage I couldn't read it anymore.

———

Deborah and Goody would consider a divorce but not an abortion. Deborah says she might be aborting the Messiah (that is a joke and not a joke). All the children claim that none of them or their friends uses pot or any other drugs. They like to listen to Cat Stevens. They speak of their Abba and Ema (father and mother) without any of the testiness and irritability common among adolescents. They don't seem threatened by the closeness of family feeling and rebellion seems unnecessary and unthinkable. There is a sweetness and a graveness to these children. I wish I could bottle it. I wish I could borrow it.

"How did the interview go?" my husband asks when I come home.

"I don't want to talk about it," I answer.

"Is something wrong?" he asks.

"No," I say, "I just feel too full of affection for strangers."

———

133

My nephew hits his forehead on the side of his bed as he stumbles in for the night.

"Be careful," says my brother.

"Yes," says my nephew, standing up in his *Star Wars* pajamas, "I remember, you told me, the head is the most important part of a little Jewish boy."

Someone had asked Rabbi Kastel about the Chasidic attitude toward skiing and swimming and baseball.

"Of course," he had said, "Jews are free to do those things, but the emphasis on the physical is Greek, not Jewish. Our emphasis is on the soul. Our work is to bring the Messiah by perfecting our spiritual selves."

"Seventeenth-century Poland pursuing us into the twentieth century," says my brother. "These people are crazies. What do they have, ten thousand perhaps? They don't believe in birth control, abortion, women's rights. They are like sheep that respond to a leader. Mitzvah mobiles, indeed."

"You don't like their singing and dancing?" I ask.

"Compared to Bach, to Mozart?" he answers. My brother is a scientist. His head is his most important part. He is not the type to go off with the Baal Shem Tov. Had he been there at the time he would have laughed. Probably I would have been dancing with the others.

———

Sunday, May 18. We go to the baseball game at Yankee Stadium. We go despite the insistent drizzle that threatens downpour. We go with umbrellas and raincoats because we are enthusiastic, old and loyal fans, and besides we had bought tickets for a benefit. Our seats, we are disappointed to find, are high up in the top decks where pigeons float comfortably an arm's length away. The seats are wet. The cement floor where we are supposed to rest our feet is several inches high in water and the level appears to be rising. The stadium lights go on although it is only two in the afternoon. The ballplayers are introduced over the loudspeakers and the Yankees take their places in the field. It's Yankee cap day. The stadium looks like an aerial view of China. (All the hats are identical and blue.) Suddenly there is a hush.

"Ladies and gentlemen, please stand for the national anthem," the loudspeaker commands. The ballplayers take off their hats and hold them solemnly over their hearts. The police by the dugouts salute the flag. Thirty thousand people remove their Yankee caps and stand up.

My daughter says, "I better not stand, my feet will get wet." She is right. If she puts her legs down she will be up to her calves in muddy rainwater.

I look out at the field with the Yankees standing in tableau, some with their heads bowed. There is a second's hush and then the opening chords are struck on some giant organ amplified enough to reach the farthest point of the most distant heaven.

"You have to stand," I say to my child, "it's a matter of respect." No sooner are the words out of my mouth than I regret them. I am making my child stand in cold, dirty water because of a ceremony my better sense mocks. I know the salaries of the ballplayers. I know all about the South Bronx and the Ku Klux Klan and Roosevelt's refusal to trade trucks for the lives of little Jewish children and about judges who were bribed and black boys swinging on magnolia trees and sweatshops and unemployment and conditions in prisons and I know they didn't mean women when they said "all men are created equal," and still I just couldn't have my child sit down when all of Yankee Stadium stood in homage to an idea, a remarkable promise, if not a reality. It is not America I dislike, a country that has offered us so much, but simplistic nationalism in whose name so many crimes have been committed the world over.

Becky stands up. I recognize I suffer from ceremony hunger. The Yankees lose the game in the tenth inning and we go home damp, cold, defeated and angry with our losing pitcher, annoyed that our seats were not as good as had been promised. In a typically American mood we went home.

———

I am on a Madison Avenue bus with my mother. I am eleven or twelve. We are going downtown to visit the dentist. His office is on the nineteenth floor of a building that has a self-service elevator. My mother doesn't trust the machinery to stop at her bidding. She expects to be hurtled to the roof or pulverized against the basement floor. She always walks up and down fire exit stairs in buildings with self-service elevators. The bus moves heavily, a prehistoric beast in a swamp. I daydream.

"See that Jewish lady over there?" my mother interrupts. I look at the row of seated figures. "The Jewish lady," she repeats. I stare a few seconds more at the row of women.

"Which one?" I ask.

"The Jewish lady in the blue dress with strawberry-blond hair and a blue hat with a veil."

"Yes, I see her," I say.

"She's dying of cancer," whispers my mother. "I can tell from looking at her."

I stare again. She is thin. She is pale and her cheeks are heavily rouged but I notice nothing special, no particular death signs. "How can you tell?" I ask my mother.

"I just can." She shrugs. "It's too hard to explain."

"How can you tell she's Jewish?" I ask.

"Can't you?" My mother seems amazed, as if I couldn't add four and four or do the three times table.

"Not exactly," I admit. Not at all in fact.

"You'll learn," she laughs, and there is something grating and bitter in her laugh, something I don't understand.

"I'm sorry," I apologize.

A little while later my mother is holding her high-heeled shoes in one hand and walking in her stockinged feet. We stop to rest on the tenth-floor landing. There is no one else in the staircase. The staircase is enclosed by decorated iron bars twisted into shapes of flowers and trees.

"Please tell me," I ask, "what makes people look Jewish?" My voice bounces off all the curlicued iron and echoes down and up all the floors.

My mother is smoking a Chesterfield cigarette. Its end is all smeared with her red lipstick. She flicks the ashes on the stone floor. She opens her bag and takes out her gold compact. Loose powder flakes about her stockinged feet. She closes her eyes when she looks in her mirror. She has a face rumpled from too little of some things and too much of others. She wipes her dark glasses with her monogrammed handkerchief. "It's no mystery," she says; "everybody can tell who is and who is not Jewish." But she doesn't add anything else. Ever since then whenever I am riding on a bus or a train I stare at all the passengers. Sometimes I think I can guess who might or might not be Jewish, but I still haven't any idea at all who is dying of cancer and who is not.

Arthur A. Cohen, novelist and Jewish scholar, says, "I love God and have mercy upon God as profoundly and as deeply as I trust God has love and mercy upon me and my children and the people of choice and the whole of creation." He says my view of God is "vulgarly naive." I wonder if there really is a path to God in the Kabbala, in the words of the Rabbi Akiba, in the work of Rashi—are there somewhere words that would take me across the obstacles and into religious conviction? I am afraid that God, if He exists, has no mercy (strained or otherwise). I am afraid of the coldness and emptiness and final obliteration I expect for myself and the generations that follow. I admire Arthur Cohen and those whose path parallels his. One of us is wrong. One of us is lost in a kind of madness, a dementia of belief. I hope fervently it is me.

———

Shortly after my article on having a Christmas tree in our home appeared in the paper, Becky developed a stomachache. It did not disappear immediately and even the most casual pat of the hand could tell she was running a fever. I was not eager to take her to our pediatrician, Dr. Samuel Soloman, a practicing traditional Jew. A rambunctious, opinionated, bossy sort of man with a determined, dedicated kind of passion that marked him off from most other doctors I knew. He was not among the svelte, sleek, quiet ones, the golfers and the collectors of art. Every time a sentence of his turns a corner it meets a Yiddish phrase. Dr. Soloman is brusque, direct and oddly gentle, and I had been a secret admirer of his for many years. His patients that crowd into the impossibly small and shabby waiting room include many from the Chasidic community in Brooklyn, as well as local blacks and Puerto Ricans and middle-class types who might have been in Scarsdale if not for some stubborn turn of mind. Dr. Soloman has politics that include active participation with groups helping Russian Jewish immigrants, and they too are often found in his office. His modern medicine coexisted with a life-style begun in the fertile crescent, shaped in the Eastern ghettos of Poland and transported almost intact to the New World. He would make house calls, but not on Saturday, unless it was an emergency. I was certain he would disapprove of me and my rather public Christmas tree and that he would be angry and say so in front of Becky. Becky was hurting in the belly and did not need to feel her mother and her doctor at odds over issues that had nothing to do with her pains, issues she had no part in designing. I put off taking her to the doctor until my maternal anxiety could bear it no longer.

We wait the usual outrageous wait. In the small room very young women in sheitels (wigs) hold tiny babies in their arms. Their breasts are full of milk. Their bodies are matronly. Their dresses, high-necked and chaste. Their shoes are sensible. Their language, Yiddish. Only their faces, as they rummaged in their bags for pacifiers and diapers, betrayed their teenage status. I stare at them rudely. I stare at the little boys of two and three wearing payess (earlocks) and yarmulkes. One of the babies starts to cry. The mother tries to comfort the infant, patting and rubbing, feeding and burping. The cries continue, insistent, demanding, grating, embarrassing because of the audience. I smile at the young mother. I remember. I remember when a baby became inconsolable and the sense of failure hung around my body like so many chains and so many stones. I catch the young mother's eye. She looks away. She does not smile. I am the unclean stranger.

At last it is our turn. Becky is undressed on the examining table. I rehearse my speech asking Samuel Soloman not to discuss my Christmas tree in front of the child. I won't let Becky take her sneakers off just in case we have to leave in a hurry.

"Take her right out of the office," said my husband, "if he brings it up."

Samuel Soloman enters the examining cubicle. He talks to Becky about her stomach. He feels her in a few places. He decides she has a virus and it will go away without the help of miracle drug or miracle doctor. He turns to me and says, "My wife Rhoda and I would like to invite you and your family to our Seder this year."

This, I understand, is his comment on my Christmas tree. I knew he'd have one.

"All of us?" I ask.

"All of you," he answers.

I am twenty years old. I am in the hospital having a minor operation. My mother has insisted that I have four large moles removed because they are the kind that can become cancerous. My mother has arranged it all. The mole on her own leg is just a few years away from its first malignant changes, but now she thinks only of the danger to her daughter. I am under the anesthetic. The surgeon is cutting here and there. What must he think of me to be in the hospital for such trivia, for the hypochondriasis of my mother? In the room where I will be wheeled when the snipping is done my mother goes through my pocketbook. She is looking for clues. Why will I not go to the country club? Why will I not wear decent clothes or even lipstick? Why will I not play cards anymore? Why have I turned down dates with any number of suitable sons of friends? Why have I taken a public vow never to have a maid or a governess? Why am I so unfriendly? She looks in my pocketbook and finds my diaphragm and the small, discreet tube of jelly. I struggle back to consciousness. I stir and open my eyes. The room turns and my stomach contracts. I am thick-tongued and search frantically among the sluggish synapses of my mind for reason, sense, self.

"You are not a virgin," my mother weeps in my ear. "You can't be married to any decent boy."

I am silent.

"Is he Jewish?" asks my mother.

I don't answer. I have broken two taboos at once. I am proud of my daring. I am also afraid, very afraid for my life. I am out of my crib, despite the bars of the hospital bed temporarily pulled up at my side. I am out of the tribe. I am an outlaw, an excommunicant, and I worry in the midst of my triumph that I might not have the nerve, the confidence, for the wide open spaces. The next day my mother goes to her astrologer who is in residence at the Little Club (a fashionable restaurant in those days). The astrologer lays out the cards on the table and tells my mother that I am having an affair with a tall, dark and handsome man. She asks me if that is true. It is true, but neither the cards nor I reveal if he is Jewish or not.

I don't remember my brother's Bar Mitzvah with any clarity at all. I do remember the hard knot of envy that sat in my chest directly between the breasts that should have been warm, nurturing and loving. I heard him stand up in the familiar synagogue on the familiar stage and read in Hebrew, but I can't recreate the whole scene in my memory. I must be indulging in repression and denial. I can hardly remember the party. I have a light memory of silver platters. He received many presents and some large checks. I pretended not to care. He was a male and his role was to take center stage, to learn, to meet the intellectual challenges, to distinguish himself in the outside world. My role was to attract a man, to look pretty enough to do the job and to behave in a docile, loving way.

"God, how I hate female lawyers," said my father. "They're so shrill and noisy and all of them are ugly."

According to Maimonides, the pious Jew has 613 commandments to fulfill. However, the Jewish woman is primarily required only to honor three: the lighting of the Shabbas candles, the baking of the Shabbas bread and the maintenance of the ritual purity of her home and her own body. God too has accepted her as maid, cook and washerwoman. In America where any boy can dream of becoming president, any girl can dream of becoming any boy, and while all feminism at that time was unconscious, still the inequality of demand did not sit well.

In the shtetl where my grandfather had grown up, in the

country where my father was born, girls stopped studying at age eight or nine and it was left to the boy to continue for a lifetime the study of Torah and of law. It was often said in the shtetl, "When the hen begins to crow like a rooster it's time to take it to the shochet [ritual slaughter]." In other words, it was unnatural for a female to seek learning, and what's more she should be killed for such perversity. My brother had obligations as a Jewish man. He now could join a minyan, whereas my presence was of no use whatsoever.

It was therefore of some comfort to me that in my parents' circle no one took this Bar Mitzvah business very seriously anyway. It hadn't mattered at all to my father and only my mother's social sense had encouraged and caused the event to be. To my cousins, aunts and uncles, the judges, lawyers and businessmen who attended, the rite was communal and had little to do with God and less to do with the Jewish forms of learning they no longer revered themselves. Only to my brother did it have spiritual meaning. I saw it in his eyes. I heard it in his voice. He cared. For a time he believed. He had actually learned the language of the Jewish intellectuals. He had understood the music of the chants and the reasons for the ritual. Even if I was a practicing atheist, a budding Socialist whose God at that time was Ernest Hemingway, I could see that my brother was not mumbling or imitating; his young soul that had already experienced so many disappointments was not disappointed in this. I have at no other day, at no other time, been that jealous of another human being. It appeared to me that he had sanctity and I had none.

Father Haig Nargesian, a large dark man, is the priest of the Episcopal church on the hill near the green in Washington, Connecticut. His stone church is one hundred yards away from the Congregational church, and two hundred yards farther down the hill rises the steeple of the Catholic church. The scene is neat, quiet, the essence of New England in spring, with forsythia growing in the yards and daffodils on the borders of each well-kept lawn. Father Haig Nargesian's grandparents were murdered by the Turks in the Armenian massacre. When he first became a priest the Anglican fathers in Boston suggested that he Americanize his name. He resisted.

"Whatever would I do with the rest of me?" he asks. Now in this Yankee village he and his children make a point of their Armenian pride. "My mother never told me the details of the massacre and I don't want to know them. I never did and I still don't. Hitler thought he could get away with the killing of the Jews because the world was silent about the Armenians. The genocides are related, you see." He went on: "I don't really understand the Jews. Why can't liberal Jews be religious? Why do liberal Jews want to appear not Jewish? The Jews are a holy and peculiar people, part of God's own design for all history. They have been chosen to keep man in his being, to keep him on holy ground."

In Father Nargesian's home in the parish house appears (collected by his wife) every brass, copper, silver object ever found at church bazaars, garage sales, fairs; every available surface is covered with teapots, candlesticks, andirons, bowls, tongs, candy dishes, cigar boxes, urns and snuffers, spoons and ladles. It is as if the Armenian were a black bull in a New England antique store where the history of America is revealed in its crafts and the objects have a purity and a unity that he with his large brooding spirit, rooted in other places, seems to be disturbing. As we sit there talking metaphysics and sociology the clock on his mantelpiece chimes away. Jew and Armenian, we are both visitors in this room.

April 1979: We go to the home of Rhoda and Samuel Soloman for the first night of the Passover. We are many. My
husband and I, my stepdaughter and daughters and a friend.
One of the Solomans' daughters is in Israel teaching but their
other daughter is with us. She is married and working as an
editorial assistant. Daniel, the Solomans' son, is teaching Jewish
history at the Ramaz School. He sits at the table, bearded,
with a yarmulke on his head, thin, intense, his fierce eyes
burning like something out of Dostoevski. We are of different
worlds. We watch each other warily. There is another family
at the Seder, a local rabbi and his wife and daughter and her
friend. There is a Soloman cousin from Detroit or Denver or
Salt Lake City. The table is very long and constructed of many
parts to sit so many people. At six thirty the books are passed
around. The reading and the prayers begin.

The Soloman family and the rabbi's family have a different
music for many of the chants. They discuss with heat which
to use with each new prayer. They arbitrate the music. The
rabbi's wife has an extraordinary voice, and listening without
the interference of knowing the meaning of the words I hear
a glorious human sound of pride and woe. The Soloman
daughter explains the meaning of each ritual to my children,
who have never been to a Seder before. The afikomen (the
ritual matzoh) is hidden. They come to the four questions. I
am afraid that as in the Seders of my childhood only the male
children will be allowed to ask the questions. I am now alert
for sexist assault. They let the girls read the questions. I am
relieved. Each of the four traditional questions is asked by a
child of different character, pictured as wise, simple, good and
wicked. The rabbi at the far end of the table explains that the
wicked child has an important function, in asking, What
does this all mean to me? he/she forces the other Jews to
explain themselves and renew their connection to the nation.
It is not so disreputable a thing, then, to ask the wicked child's
question. There is a tradition for it.

The prayers go on. The telling of the story of the exodus

goes on. I am mesmerized by the sound of the incomprehensible Hebrew and by the weight of the story of liberation. I think like all the others at the table of the centuries and centuries of Jewish families who have sat as we are sitting and who have told the story as it is told and it is hard to remain rational and distant. I am caught by the drama of the slave against the free.

I listen for the door to open to let Elijah in.

I remember as a child staring at the cup, wondering if Elijah had really entered the room and taken his portion. I puzzled about how even an angel could be everywhere at once. (Santa Claus poses the same metaphysical problem.) All the grown-ups laughed and teased. To a child, of course, God's presence or absence in the home is no laughing matter. Now as my children open the front door of the Soloman house I cannot resist a quick look at the wine goblet at the center of the table. To atone for this absurd regression I remind myself of all the innocent Egyptians who died that the Jews might flee and I remain hardened against the God who chose this people and inflicted so much on them. I do not forgive. I drink my wine at the right moments but I cannot help hating this God who shows such neglect, who has betrayed His covenant, hate Him for His destructiveness, for the serpent in the garden, for the suffering of Job, for the diabolical unfolding of His vicious grand plans, for the humiliations He forces on mankind. I forgive nothing even while I doubt the existence of anything more than random atoms crashing about into black holes and connecting with significant gases.

My little children grow dazed and sleepy. They are learning that boredom is the handmaiden of ritual, that the human need for ceremony leads to the human need to escape from the communal to the private, even to sleep. The food is served, simple and good. The conversation turns to points of observance, different ways of singing the same prayer, different shades and hairs of habits. The songs are sung more and more vibrantly, gustily. The room is heavy with childhood memories that we as strangers can only imagine. My older children are looking at their watches. Is this evening going to take forty years? they are wondering. My children look for the matzoh. (Traditionally at the beginning of the Seder a piece of matzoh is blessed and hidden. The children look for it later and receive a gift from the head of the household when they find the matzoh. The Seder cannot continue till the children return the matzoh.) The little girls are so tired by now that they need help in finding it. Rhoda is in the kitchen, Samuel is at the head of the table. I hope that my children don't notice that. My husband is quiet. The flight from Egypt leads for him to the ovens of Dachau, to the smallness of mind and the narrowness of opportunity of his parents' life. He is not completely charmed, but he is patient because the occasion means so much to our kind hosts. Even if the invitation stemmed from some variety of missionary impulse that is not such an evil thing.

He is less of a romantic than I. He carries the contradictions, the unresolved questions of our spiritual life with more stoic courage than I do. This night he thinks of his mother, who tried to keep a kosher home but was undone by her scoffing husband. He is quiet at the Seder. He is in the company of certain memories.

We read a passage about the Holocaust. We recite a prayer for the Russian Jews who are in the midst of a struggle for their own exodus. The lines of good and bad are sharply drawn and there is no question that the struggle has been long and the suffering heavy, and that only a coward or a moral fool would prefer to join the oppressors rather than the voice filled with dignity and beauty of the victim. The Seder seems like a long pledge of allegiance in which each person at the table joins in the reading and in the prayers and in so doing commits, connects himself to the flood tides of Jewish history, binds himself again to the tribe. I feel the pull of the ancient rituals and I pull back. The wine, the music, the rhythms of the repeated prayers, they are a kind of hocus-pocus clouding my reason, my good sense, my independence, my universality. Despite myself the distances close. I am not such a stranger to this place.

The readings resume after dessert. My little children are sitting upright in their chairs as if suspended by strings. They are no longer absorbing what is happening. It is quarter to one in the morning.

On the drive home our youngest child falls asleep. The others are wondering about all the disagreements about the songs for the different rituals. They are so assimilated that they don't understand that tension and argument are the natural landscape of the service, part of the Jewish experience. On the way home I decide I am the "wicked child" and I will ask my questions.

Several weeks later the prize for finding the afikomen comes in the mail for the children. The youngest receives a Jewish history book and the ten-year-old a book on the Holocaust. She reads it in a day and then goes to the library and gets more books on the Holocaust and afterward more. Because I accepted an invitation to that Seder my daughter Katie has a different childhood than she might otherwise.

———

Our psychoanalyst friend Dr. Martin Bergmann has written a review in the *Psychoanalytic Quarterly* of a book called *From Oedipus to Moses, Freud's Jewish Identity*. Martin Bergmann quotes from the book: "There is a letter from Kafka to his friend Max Brod which says, 'The father complex from which more than one Jew draws his spiritual nourishment relates not to the innocent father but to the father's Judaism.' What most of those who began to write in German wanted was to break with Judaism, generally with the vague approval of their fathers (this vagueness is the revolting part). That is what they wanted, but their hind legs were bogged down in their father's Judaism and their front legs could find no new ground. The resulting despair was their inspiration."

This applies to American Jewish writers as well, to Mike Gold, Delmore Schwartz, both Roths, to Saul Bellow, to Bernard Malamud. For them the generational struggle, the move away from the home and its claims, the path to assimilation and enlightenment created feelings of guilt, anger and, of course, anxiety. For most, of course, whose hind legs were stuck in Brownsville and Crown Heights, Newark or the Bronx, whose front legs pawed the air in frantic motions, inspiration did not come. They lived or live their lives suspended and vulnerable. It's an impossible position to hold; like being in a wheelchair, it causes further debilitation. Kafka's despair can lead to more despair instead of to art. People can be miserable without being writers.

In America, sons regarded their father's Judaism with a jaundiced eye, but daughters, late, last, only recently have begun to struggle in just the same way against their mother's Judaism. The feminine waving of front legs about in the air required further assimilation since the more traditional the Jewish woman was, the less likely she would be to have a full traditional Talmudic education. While women were sometimes offered a secular education, their opportunities to strive toward the larger world were limited. Eventually the Jewish woman did begin to speak, forming a ridiculously high percentage of the women's movement. Not all geniuses, to be sure, but contributors just the same. They complained and cajoled against their Jewish backgrounds that, like a chastity belt, could neither be removed nor worn in comfort. Among them we count Tillie Olsen, Grace Paley, Lois Gould, Alix Kates Shulman, Betty Friedan, Erica Jong, Susan Brownmiller. All of them sisters of Gluckel, but because of their greater emancipation they wanted more than to record, they wanted to create change.

In Connecticut every time the phone rings my skin pulls tight over my skull. My hands begin to sweat. I am afraid they're calling from the day camp where Becky is endlessly riding a horse to tell me that she has fallen, been stepped upon, has a concussion, a broken limb, or worse. When the caller is only a friend, a wrong number, a bill collector, I am instantly relieved and ashamed of my earlier anxiety.

For the most part Jews in the shtetl left animals alone. They were the concern and care of the goyim. My mother hated cats with a deep passion. She told me they would suffocate little babies if they were given a chance. My mother was afraid of dogs. She didn't admire their strong bodies, their soft fur, the sweetness and affection in their eyes. She thought only about their teeth and their savage impulses. She thought with horror of their obvious and constant display of biological functioning. Dogs and cats were not for her. Horses, they were beyond the pale both literally and figuratively. They were beasts who relieved themselves at will, dangerous beasts with urges to kick, rear, to gallop and bite. My mother was not touched by the relationship of the human animal to the others. (Although, I am told, Rabbi Kook, the first chief rabbi of Israel, rode everywhere on horseback or camel.) My mother considered it one of the duties of her life to hide, disguise, repress, suppress her own animalness.

My mother was not an admirer of free motion. She was corseted, garter-belted, high-heeled, painted, waxed, coiffed, plucked. She was not one to run in the breeze like a deer or climb a tree like a squirrel. She swam in heated pools with a careful sidestroke; she kept her bathing-capped head raised above the water to protect her hairdo. Part of my rebellion was a love of dogs, an admiration of cats, a willingness to clean litter boxes and walk dogs down city streets, to comb and

ANNE ROIPHE

brush and touch animals. Let them scratch the furniture, let them soil the carpets. I am on the side of the animals against the trappings of respectable life. We are a family of two cats and two dogs.

"Excessive," says my stepdaughter, who finds my rebellions quaint and old-fashioned.

But horses! Becky rides in the Connecticut horse shows in a velvet hard hat, in a jacket and jodhpurs and black boots. She might not be recognizable to her great-grandmother. My mother would have fainted dead away to see her take the two-and-a-half-foot jumps. The truth of the matter is that enough of my mother survives in me so that I faint away also. I just don't allow it to show. I want my daughters to be water skiers, snow skiers, ballplayers, hikers, discus throwers, joggers. I want them to have Hellenic spirits. I do not want to think of them waiting for the Madison Avenue bus in high-heeled shoes, carrying home little white boxes of cakes for the taste of husbands and children. My mother told me not to take a bath while menstruating; it could cause infection. She told me not to take gym while menstruating; it could cause damage to the important inner organs. She thought black cats were un-lucky and dogs' saliva carried polio germs. Becky loves horses. At this time of year she rides fast through meadows filled with black-eyed Susans and purple thistles. I follow her with my anxieties. It's her choice. Assimilation is about change. For centuries in the shtetl, mothers, daughters and granddaughters did the same thing, led the same life. Now we can depend only on the inevitability of change.

Isaac B. Singer has written a masterpiece called *The Magician of Lublin*. Among other things it is a story of attempted and failed assimilation. Yasha, who is an escape artist, a self-taught Houdini, an acrobat and a performer of enormous talent, has a loyal, trusting wife in the shtetl named Esther. She waits patiently for him during the many months of his long trips about the country. Esther is long-suffering, good, pious and has a small role in the story as Singer wrote it. Yasha, the rebel, who has long avoided shul, who consorts with gamblers and gangsters, has a mistress, his Polish Gentile assistant who helps him with his act and takes care of him on their long tours. Her name is Magda. She is dumb and long-suffering also. She, too, loves him with complete devotion and loyalty. In Warsaw, Yasha seeks not only fame as an artist but the love of Emilia, a high-class woman, the widow of a Polish professor. He thinks he is truly in love with this image of high society, of education, of the open world, far from the shtetl of his birth and of his waiting wife, Esther. Emilia wants to go to Italy with him, away from the provincialism of his village, even from Poland itself, and have him perform for the kings and queens of Europe. For this they need money. Ready to abandon both his wife and his mistress, Yasha tries to steal the money, but for the first time in his life his physical skills and his wit fail him. His conscience or his roots betray him and he falls to the ground literally and symbolically. He ends up with fever, fear and self-loathing. He returns to his rooms in Warsaw and finds that his Polish mistress Magda has hanged herself in despair over his infidelity and impending desertion. His guilt expands over the edges of hysteria.

Beaten and defeated in his grand ambitions to deny and flee his original place in God's world, he returns to the shtetl. Esther has a small dressmaking business and is able to support him. In their yard he builds himself a tiny, bricked-in hut with no door and only a small window to the outside. He stays in this hut with a straw pallet, a shovel for burying excrement and a Bible. He prays day and night and studies the Torah. As the months go by he gains the reputation of a holy man and rabbis and students of rabbis come to ask his advice and to discuss God with him. He is as gifted in his role as saint as he was as a performer. Esther brings him his meals and his mail and so the book ends. The irony of the parable ripples on and on. Yasha's fate may reflect that of the Chasidic Jewry of Poland who turned inward to God and secluded themselves in their shuls and so missed the chance to escape the coming catastrophe of the Holocaust. Disaster and sainthood are always related, if not identical twins. Yasha returns to his religion, to his Yiddish roots, because escape artist that he was he could not do the impossible, escape from his childhood, deny his Jewishness and leave his tribe. Yasha makes of his return a victory, a spiritual ecstasy of reunion. He is spectacular in his defeat.

But the further irony is that this victory was built on the suffering of others: mistress, widow and, of course, the doubly deserted wife (once for other women and then for God). There is ghastly irony in the description of this Houdini of the Jews imprisoning himself in a shack, laying on the phylacteries, growing the beard. He could escape from any chains except that of religion. Is the way to God always through a prison? When he renounced lust, renounced sex all together, renounced drink and pleasure, he became holy, except he may now be more of an immoral monster than ever before. His devoted childless wife Esther is left alone in bed, comfortless through the long nights, alone to make a living through the day. She has a holy man in her yard but no husband, no friend or companion, no place to release her tenderness, her sex. In becoming such a blessed person Yasha struggled with Satan to maintain his faith. He chastises himself as a beast that must stay in a cage. He engages in long dialogues with God, mortifying his flesh and wallowing in the long list of his previous sins. In doing this he denies Esther the simple comforts of life. Does Singer care? It is hard to know because the use of women as foils in a man's spiritual journey has become so legitimate a part of our literary tradition that it may now be all but unconscious.

It may seem rude and ridiculous to add to a work of such amazing quality, but The Magician of Lublin has exactly the quality of a legend. It is the kind of story that turns into public property. The success of this tale encourages the audiences' imagination and invites them to play. I am certain that I. B. Singer would be the last person to take offense at a daydream.

This is how I would like the book to end:

Yasha read his letter from Emilia. He read and reread the part where she expressed her admiration for his religious reputation. He was astonished that she had survived his downfall and desertion. He remembered the curve of her breasts and he could feel in his hands the round bottom of her daughter Halina, that must now be rounder and riper than ever. He paced back and forth in his small cell. He stared out the narrow window through which Esther had just handed him the letter. The day was cold and clear. If he moved himself around in his cell, pressing his body flat to the wall, he could see each corner of the yard, the clean snow that by this afternoon would be trampled by his rabbinical visitors. Would there come a time when his penitence would be over? Had the Mercy of the Creator sent him this letter from Emilia as a signal, as a sign, like the dove with an olive branch? Had God seen the efforts of His child Yasha and was he ready to send him back into the world of the living? Yasha turned round and round in excited circles. His body had lost its strength in his internment. He became dizzy with the effort. Perhaps this letter (his hope) was only another of Belial's tricks, a ruse to distract him from God's own path and lead him out of his shelter and back into temptation. He would wait and see. The snowflake he had examined in the morning, the magnificent hexagonal shape with patterns designed in God's own mind, it had melted on his windowsill and disappeared. He immediately dropped to his knees, praying to God to forgive him his half-articulated wish to live forever, to hold on to his mortal shape and soul till the end of days and beyond.

Meanwhile Esther, who had not delivered this letter with strange feminine handwriting (postmarked Warsaw) without first steaming it open and satisfying herself about its contents, was busy in the kitchen with preparations of her own. Her heart beat very loudly. She repeated the prayers of her childhood over and over again. She felt cold and wore on her thin shoulders every shawl she possessed. She had brought Yasha his rice and milk and had smiled at him warmly. It was the first time in a long while that she did not have a sourness in her voice or her eyes. Yasha did not know her well enough to distinguish the appearance of kindness from the reality. The day was a Friday, which suited her plans exactly. If God had not meant to help her, she thought, He would have made the day Tuesday or Thursday. She would then have had to wait and perhaps in that waiting grow frightened and change her mind. She dismissed her assistants early that day on the premise of wanting to prepare an extra sweet for Yasha on the Sabbath.

When the students had left his little window and their footprints were dirty smudges on the clean snow, Esther gathered the bricks from the garden wall that had been permitted (since no man worked about the house) to fall in a pile on the ground. She took the extra bag of cement left by the workers who had built Yasha's cell on that day that had caused her such grief and sent her into a loneliness that had opened the doors for demons to come at night when she lay in bed and touch her in places that were sacred and private. Everyone knows that demons feel free to take liberties with women discarded by their husbands. The worthless of this world are gifts to the worthless of the next.

Esther prepared her cement in her cooking pots. She decided not to use her milk pots, not wanting also to offend the laws of kashruth. As the darkness settled in, she paused to light the Sabbath candles as she had every Sabbath since she had left her mother's home. How many Sabbaths had she sat down alone with the Sabbath Queen who passed quickly enough through such a barren house? Tonight she pushed her wheelbarrow out to Yasha's hut. She made several trips back and forth to the garden wall. Yasha was deep in prayer. He paid no attention to her. He had learned to avoid looking at her when she came and peered at him through the window, staring at him with large complaining eyes. She went to the house and carried out her pots and a thick knife she would need for spreading.

Yasha lay down on his straw pallet, exhausted by the unexpected thoughts that had besieged him as a result of Emilia's letter. He heard the scrapings and the sound of thumping as brick hit brick but he paid no attention as he had trained himself to do. He listened to his inner voices only. Soon he was in a deep sleep, untormented for once. A sign he would have taken for God's understanding had the circumstances in which he woke up been different. Esther, remembering that Yasha had once been an escape artist, bricked in the entire wall and covered the lower rims of the other sides as well.

The day after the Sabbath she explained to the rabbi and the visiting pilgrims and her assistants how Yasha had taken a sudden fever and begged her as he was dying to turn his cell into a coffin after he died. It was irregular, of course, but Yasha had always been irregular and now he was such a holy person that the rabbi had to accept his wishes in death. The rabbi spent some hours over his books and found the words in an ancient Babylonian tractate that permitted such an odd burial. The hut would have become a kind of object of wonder, a Jewish shrine, if the local Chasidim (who had been jealous of the attention Yasha had taken from their own rabbi) had not claimed that one of them had a dream in which an angel told them that Yasha's soul was safe but his sins lingered by the hut and could do harm to passersby. That stopped the traffic through Esther's yard fast enough, and she was grateful.

———

I do not know what frightens Samuel and Rhoda Soloman in their dreams. I do not know what disappointments they have given each other. I do not know what their marriage has eroded away, and beyond everything, I do not know what their lives would have been like if they had chosen different directions in early years. This brief description is only from the outside; the inner landscape, the most interesting one to travel, is beyond the borders where I have no passport and my guesses and fantasies remain just that, guesses and fantasies. More importantly I see them as a family, parents, grandparents, children, superimposed on a screen of my own family, needs of mine float to the surface and interfere with objective reporting. Reason alone cannot entirely subdue the yearnings for closeness I feel while talking to them.

Rhoda is a large woman with a sweet smile. She looks exactly the part of the Jewish mother. She is buxom, strong, solid, a kind of beauty that perhaps went out of style with the turn of the century. Her flesh weighs her down but her eyes have a certain fire, sureness, a kind of shy confidence. Passing her on the street one might notice only a middle-aged matron who is doing her duty, but looking carefully there is an unexpected lightness, a sharpness of mind and a tenderness of soul, much used, perhaps somewhat abused, but a tenderness ready and quick.

Rhoda's parents came from Russia in 1906. Her mother and father were both seventeen years old and met in America at the Socialist Farbend. They were not religious. They were among the rebellious young people on the Lower East Side who went to Yom Kippur balls. Her father had been trained in Russia as a ritual slaughterer, but he wanted something else in his new life in the New World. He had no secular education but still he could quote all of Pushkin. He had read all the Hebrew secular literature and quoted poetry to his children all the time.

When Rhoda's parents married they moved to Brownsville, and her father became a cutter in a ladies' lingerie factory. Both parents remained active Socialists, although her mother also lit the candles on the Sabbath and baked the challah bread. All of the children were sent to the Hebrew school on the corner. Rhoda and Samuel both remember standing as young children on the top of the subway steps holding out little blue paper boxes and asking for money for Palestine. They would bring their boxes to school and the money raised would be sent to the new settlements. All the children in the neighborhood had little blue boxes and the grown-ups talked and argued over the finer points of Zionism and Socialism. Rhoda's parents spoke Yiddish and knew Hebrew and Russian. Rhoda describes the Sabbath in her home when all the aunts and uncles and cousins would stop in for the midday meal or during the afternoon for tea and there would be endless talk and reciting of poetry and political arguments. Most of the family lived within walking distance of one another.

Samuel's parents came from Russia to the Lower East Side when they were children. Samuel's grandfather was a learned man who personally taught the Bar Mitzvah to each of his five sons' sons. For six months every evening he would come to their house or have them visit him in Williamsburg in Brooklyn. He would teach the readings of the Torah but he also taught Yiddishkeit, morals and customs and traditions. He understood the pressures on his grandchildren in America and, although he was a very pious and Orthodox man, he gave Samuel permission to play basketball on Saturday since that was his one day off from school and studying. He allowed him not to wear the kepah in the street since that made his grandson uncomfortable. Samuel's mother attended the Jewish Theological Seminary and became a Hebrew teacher. She also was one of the earliest Hebrew typists. His father worked for many years at the Hebrew Free Loan Society, an organization that now has two of their sons on its board of directors. The entire family moved to Crown Heights. In Crown Heights, in the days when the Soloman boys were growing up, everything was Jewish. There were big synagogues and little synagogues and the Soloman family belonged to the largest of them all, The Brooklyn Jewish Center. The Rabbi Israel Leventhal was, says Samuel, "a great sermonizer and a wonderful man who knew and cared about every one of the two thousand families at the center." Now he is ninety-two years old and Samuel and Rhoda still keep in touch with him.

While Samuel went to Townsend Harris High, because his father wanted him to have a secular education, he also attended the Herzlia on the Lower East Side. This was a Hebrew school where the students went three nights a week from six to ten, after their regular school. Here they learned Hebrew poetry and read and discussed Hebrew novels. They studied the prophets and the Commentaries and of course Zionism. At fifteen Samuel and Rhoda were in the same class at the Herzlia and Samuel teases Rhoda, "The reason I sat next to her, to be perfectly honest, was not because she was good-looking or rich. She was neither. She was by far the best Talmud student in the class." Samuel laughs. He adds, "She was the most beautiful girl in the world."

"Our daughter," Rhoda interrupts, "now teaches Talmud in Israel. Probably there are not more than a half-dozen women in America and Israel who know enough Talmud to teach it. When I attended the Herzlia it was revolutionary for boys and girls to learn together. We had a wonderful education and met many interesting people."

"Those teachers," Samuel explains, "were different from the yeshiva teachers of our earlier childhood. These teachers were the products of the Haskala, the enlightenment."

Samuel left the Herzlia when he went on to medical school; he could no longer carry the two programs. Rhoda continued at the Herzlia when she went to Brooklyn College and then to Hebrew teachers college. She went to Brooklyn during the day and to the Herzlia in the evenings and she did her reading on the subway and never got home before eleven o'clock at night. Rhoda also practiced the piano from seven to eight in the morning.

Samuel had always wanted to be a doctor and he remembers conversations with his "sainted grandfather" who steered his grandsons away from the rabbinate. He wanted them to be learned but to enter the secular world. Samuel's grandfather said to him when he was a boy, "I know you want to be a doctor. It's a very grave responsibility. You will take the responsibility of having people's lives in your hands. If you do it, please remember your tradition; you don't decide everything. There are some things God decides."

Samuel adds, "That's pretty corny, but let me tell you I tell that to medical students to this day."

Rhoda says, "The common thread that ran through both our families, though they didn't know each other, was a love for Jewish learning, for continuing Jewish studies, more than ritual observance. It was very important for both families to maintain the link to Jewish learning. In both families, aunts and uncles had been scholars and high-school teachers." Rhoda had an uncle who was an important Judaica scholar.

Rhoda says that her family's Seders always had thirty or forty people at them. "One of my mother's sisters lived upstairs in the same brownstone in Brownsville. My cousins and my family were always together in either house as though we were one family."

Samuel adds that his other grandfather and his aunt and uncle lived directly across the street and every kind of holiday was an excuse for the whole family to celebrate together. Samuel says that of his father's four brothers they all lived in Brooklyn except for one who moved to Washington Heights in Manhattan and the whole family wondered. They blamed his wife.

All of the children on Samuel's and Rhoda's generational line have remained religious. Rhoda has one sister in Salt Lake City who imports her kosher meat from Denver. She is the pillar of the Jewish community in Salt Lake. She teaches Hebrew school.

"All my family and Samuel's have maintained kosher homes," said Rhoda.

Samuel says that he and "all my brothers went to a Jewish

camp called Cejwin, a Reconstructionist camp under the influence of Mordecai Kaplan. The clientele of the camp was mixed, Orthodox, Conservative, secular. We were exposed to all points of view. It was an act of genius on my father's part to send us there. All of our children, my brothers' and mine, have gone to the same camp. None of them lost anything of their own beliefs. On the contrary, they think they influenced some kids to be more traditional."

Rhoda says that not until college did she have a Christian friend, and she has lost touch with her. Samuel says that he had Christian friends at Townsend Harris. He had a Christian constituency and they worked very hard to help him be elected president of the school. Samuel started at Brooklyn College and then switched to New York University because there was no other way to get into medical school.

"The financial sacrifice my father had to make to send me to NYU must have been extraordinary," he says. Samuel was a resident at Brooklyn Jewish in pediatrics and from there went to Massachusetts General for three years. Their first child was born in Massachusetts.

Samuel and Rhoda do feel that they are ecumenical within the Jewish world. They feel they have very strong commitments to their tradition but they resist precise labeling.

Rhoda says, "We always had the Zionist dream. Even in 1906 when my parents came to America they had friends who went to Palestine. We dreamed of a Zionist state. We didn't think in the 1940s about going there."

Samuel adds, "It seemed such an impossibility then to actually go and live there. We had friends who did go live in kibbutzim. But we had so much family here. If I had it to do all over again, knowing what I know now, I might have considered it more seriously. Who ever thought of uprooting ourselves? Travel seemed so far and difficult, only the radical kids actually went. My friends who went are now big wheels in Israel."

Samuel talks about the Saturdays of his childhood. "You

always looked forward to the end of the week. You knew Saturday was coming. I know it was the same in Rhoda's house. It smelled different. My mother cooked different food. When you woke up Friday morning everything felt different. You couldn't wait to get home Friday night. The gefilte fish was always standing in platters and in fact we would often sneak all the gefilte fish before supper. On Friday night we all ate together. (My father couldn't eat with us during the week.) We would go to service and then we would come home and sing together and we would have long political discussions. Now the cycle has repeated itself. My father would criticize his sons for being too liberal and we would say he was too conservative, the same things our children tell us now. We would go to service on Saturday and then we had long leisurely lunches and guests and family came by all day long. On the Sabbath you should eat three meals. Friday night is the first meal, lunch is the second, and then Saturday evening you had a third, cold meal, bagels, lox and tea. We always shared the Saturday meals with friends and relatives. We had long discussions about labor unions, Communists, Socialists, about who was running for office. There was always a lot of shouting. It is still that way now in our house in Riverdale, only there are not so many relatives around."

Samuel and Rhoda's synagogue is the one that Rabbi Greenberg had led until he began to teach at City College. The Soloman children, like two of the Greenberg children, were sent to the Ramaz School in Manhattan and on to the yeshiva. Sarah, the older Soloman daughter who is now in Israel, went to Harvard for a master's in education. Daniel and his married sister Sharon are in the midst of thinking and rethinking about their relationship to each of the traditional rituals they were brought up with. At this writing Daniel has left the teaching of Jewish history and is reconsidering a career in medicine. He is working as a psychiatric research aide in a state hospital. Sharon is writing for a magazine called *Working Woman*.

Rhoda has joined the Jewish Federation Task Force on the

Role of Jewish Women, a feminist organization that hopes to have impact within the Jewish community. Rhoda is a feminist who hopes that in the near future the female position will change in all the Jewish congregations. This makes Samuel laugh and admit he's not quite ready for it. In principle yes, but . . .

Samuel and Rhoda have been deeply involved with the Soviet Jews that have come to America, and almost every year since 1971 they have traveled to the Soviet Union, visiting and encouraging the Jewish community there. They have carried in Jewish material and taken out letters. They are personally involved in the fate of this last Jewish remnant whose religion and identity are repressed in the Soviet Union. Samuel treats free of charge the children of the newly arrived Russian immigrants. Sometimes he speaks to them in Yiddish, sometimes in a halting Russian.

I am in the office waiting for him to check Katie for a school form. I see him enter an examining room where a grandmother, mother and baby are waiting. I overhear the young mother apologizing for her baby's lack of records and absence of proper vaccinations.

"He was not born here," says the mother in heavily accented English.

"He's like us, then," said Samuel. "Everyone in America was more or less born someplace else. He'll do fine. He's one of us." The young mother translates this into Russian and both women laugh.

CONCLUSIONS

Preface to the Conclusions

These conclusions are both tentative and personal and not meant as prescriptions or instructions. We all approach this subject with our particular childhood memories and these lead us in different directions. We have strong affections or distastes, we are in accord with our parents or in reaction. We have as small children accepted the primal connection to religion or race and made it as fundamental a part of ourselves as our gender sense, our private body image, or we have pushed it aside, connected it only superficially to ourselves, an attribute like eye color or foot size. For varieties of reasons mostly personal and part of each individual psychological path, we have either tried to live within our place or escaped or partially escaped or tried to escape and failed.

No one of us has found the way to a perfect life and we can only respect each other's search. Jews and Christians must know that gracious acceptance of the differences in others is the minimal, most urgent, rule of civilized people anywhere.

In Flatbush where my husband was raised, the world of Eastern Jewry stretched as far as the eye could see and the feet could walk. Only the schoolteachers were visitors from other lands. The school itself was like a great airport set deep in the hills of some foreign and backward country. From this airport one could embark for Mozart and Bach, for Darwin and Einstein, for Thomas Mann and Goethe, for Emerson and Thoreau, for Jane Austen and the Bronte sisters, for Keats and Dante and T. S. Eliot. From those runways you could travel to Manhattan to universities, from the particular to the universal, from the Gemeinschaft to the Gesellschaft, to medicine, to law, to art and dental school and accounting classes, to wealth and security beyond one's parents' fondest dreams. The schools were free, of course, but a price had to be paid. In the rambling shtetl of Flatbush the Jewish children were taught the old country tale of their superiority to the goyim, superiority of a moral and intellectual sort, and they held over the absent heads of the goyim the sanctity of the age-old victim who has in his worldlessness had time to develop sharpness of wit and reveal to himself levels upon levels of soul. They believed the old country rumors, what was goyish was brutish, dumb and unclean. Gentile women were taboo.

Nevertheless there was a certain hidden agenda to all this pride. Why if the Jews are so extraordinary is their history one of helplessness, martyrdom and exodus? Why if the Gentile is so simple a creature do the world and the school belong to him and we are the temporary guests, the pariahs and the parvenus? In Flatbush, Crown Heights, Brownsville, and the Concourse many were wondering: Why are the great civilizations we learn about in the schools not ours? It was well known to the Jews of the American ghettos, as the *Fortune* magazine article on anti-Semitism (February 1936) stated, Jews had no part of major industry in this country, an infinitesimal role in the arena of high finance and were proportionately underrepresented in newspapers, radio and advertising. Whatever the anti-Semites might feel, Jews controlled very little, although their distinctiveness made them as always, everywhere, subject of discussion, object of fear and their power romanticized into a "Jewish question" or a "Jewish problem." They knew all that in the ghettos and they were also puzzled by the paradox of the shiksa. Why if she is so stupid, bland and forbidden is she also so attractive? (My husband spent his boyhood dreaming about Ingrid Bergman and Myrna Loy.) My husband taught himself to speak without an identifiable Brooklyn or Jewish accent through these same movies. His speech patterns no longer resemble those of his father or brother.

Part of the price paid to leave the ghetto was some shame, some doubt; some narcissistic injury was suffered, nurtured in self-consciousness, bred in observations of Gentile America as revealed in movies, books and radio. The other part of the ticket out was purchased with the loneliness of separation. The separation that followed naturally when you no longer spoke the language of your parents and the siblings you left behind.

My husband's father Albert was a round-faced, small man who always carried candy in his pockets for the neighborhood black and Puerto Rican children. In his last years he would sit for hours in the parks in Washington Heights and watch the children roller skating and playing ball. For him the American dream, the streets of gold, had not quite worked out. His endless series of jobs and opportunities seemed always to terminate in repeated financial catastrophe. But for his educated son the story was different. The father had pride in his American-born son that by its very nature could not be reciprocated. His victory was that his son was a stranger.

My husband's father would come to our house when he was in his early seventies and we were newly married. He would sit politely with us for a while and there would be great silences, dead spots in the conversations that no degree of small talk could cover. He would go off and talk with the children and tell them tales of pogroms, of long, anguishing cheder lessons, of going barefoot in the winter snows of

Odessa, of being impressed into the czar's army and running away to America. When my father-in-law died in his small apartment near the George Washington Bridge, there was among his few possessions a shoe box in which he had collected every one of his son's report cards from the great airport school. He had saved the second-grade teacher's comments and the high-school teacher's letter on awarding a science prize and all the yellow cards covered with gold stars that had been his pride, his naches, his yichus, had represented his son, been in fact an effigy of his son in his son's psychological absence.

The great migrations set off by the pogroms of the late nineteenth century changed the world's distribution of Jews. In 1850 there were five thousand Jews in America and millions in Eastern Europe. By 1920, when the immigration wave was forced to subside, there were millions in America. And after Hitler, now in 1980, about five thousands Jews remain in Poland and Hungary. It is hard to think of oneself as part of a historical movement, as a particle in the historical tides. It is definitely hard to think of oneself like Neolithic man or the primitive horse crossing the Azores and leaving skeletons in caves that reveal travels of great distances. We are so filled with the particulars of our egos, the distinctiveness of our organism, that it becomes almost painful to shift back and see oneself as mass, subject to prevailing winds and product of social forces that gave no quarter to our uniqueness.

I had thought of myself as having chosen to be assimilated, as having rejected the synagogue and substituted my college education for the education of the Sunday school. I had thought of the disconnections of my life as preludes to the new connections that were mine by choice. Some truth in all that, but some illusion also. Rebel that I was pretending to be, I was in fact like a salmon swimming upstream at the appropriate time of year, merely doing what comes naturally. The emancipation of the Jews that followed Napoleon's travels about Europe allowed a reach for a more secure economic life, a reach for the growing technologies, the sciences and the arts that were at the time enriching all the Western world, and drew the Jews (like the great natural migrations of swan and swallow) into the mainstream. Moses Mendelssohn, humpbacked but brilliant, made his contributions to Berlin society, and his children, unprotected by superstition, fear of the Gentile, reached for the gold ring, not merely assimilation but absorption into the Christian universe, to become idolaters, apostates, social arrivists, breakers of ancient taboos and explorers of new social dimensions.

From the pariahs that their grandparents had been, that Gluckel herself had been, they became educated, civilized, nonauthentic, parvenus, hypocrites, imitators, masked creatures whose real faces had worn off under the masks and might now be blank, but simultaneously the world was open to them. They became wealthy, educated in many languages, polished, followers of the arts and the social sciences, musicians, performers. Escape artists they may have been, they no longer jumped off the sidewalks to let the Gentile pass. They were partakers of the feast of culture, a prepared feast of its own. It was a trade, it had advantages and disadvantages.

Because of accidents of geography, because it took 150 years for the process of the tearing down of the ghetto walls to occur, because it required persecutions of an intense sort to break up the little villages of Eastern Jewry, my parents and grandparents and my husband's parents were all relatively new to the process of emancipation, for them the enlightenment came late. We are as a family, in flux, in change, within the generational levels as well as one generation against the other. The gilded ghetto of my childhood with its country clubs, its dancing schools, its own private school system, its demands for conformity, its repression of female aspiration, its materialism that grew like a monster till finally it ate up all the time and energy at least of its women who were eternally in the stores, worn out from shopping, from trips to fabric houses, carpet stores, whose days were filled with fancy slipcovers that had been sent in the wrong colors and purchases for resort wear that had to be just right—that ghetto was not a resting place for many generations. The children who swam in the swimming pool with me went on to marry Gentile men or professors of foreign languages or revolutionaries. Those, the duller sort, who stayed to marry the good Jewish businessmen and join the clubs in turn, in middle age have gotten divorces and gone back to school and learned a trade. They are now speech therapists and marriage counselors. They do pottery and paint. One I know left her family in Westchester to work with alcoholics on an Indian reservation in Omaha.

There are ironic twists to this social movement. My parents' world of golf and canasta, of multiple Irish and German servants, of Palm Beach and Atlantic Beach, of manufacturers who learned to water-ski and lawyers who learned how to play the right political game in the city of scandal, was bordered on all sides with rules of dress, rules of behavior and constant demands that one stay within the group. But even as those demands were being made the group was dissolving and changing shape. Its children became possessed by other matters. The country clubs, the schools did not all disappear. Others, newer to economic comfort, came to take the empty places. This assimilation process is a little like a parade, a long, huge parade with the German Jews in the front and the Sephardic Jews in the reviewing stands and the long, long line of Ostjude stretching back a way. Naturally each person's individual experience with moving out of the ghetto, into the world of the emancipation, will depend on what year he is where, where his parents were on the parade route. There is room for odd maverick choices: one can move in the opposite direction of the parade, one can appear to leave the route altogether by joining a Hare Krishna group or becoming a High Episcopalian, one can take a long ride in the Lubavitcher mitzvah mobile. But for the majority of us, our manners, our style, our language, the ones we have forgotten and the ones we pretend to have never heard, the ones we are learning, vary according to our forward motion on this line, on the parade route.

When I went to a predominantly Gentile high school I became ashamed of my mother, whose clothes and manner were different from most of the other mothers', who wore oxford shoes with their blue stockings and understated tweeds over bodies that had played golf and done volunteer social work for generations. It was a matter of class mixed with ethnicity. I understood none of it. I experienced shame and shame for my shame, for even a child knows snobbery for what it is, and especially a child understands primary loyalties to group and tribe. It would have comforted me to have known that both Dr. Helene Deutsch and Rosa Luxemburg also felt shame and anger at their bourgeois mothers.

Now as an adult certain things are much clearer. I slip-slided, I inched, I backed up into the intellectual, left-wing, primarily Jewish (though for most the Jewish part is not very consciously relevant) class. My children went on peace marches as babies. They were pushed through museums as soon as the paintings were at eye level. They have been taught to gather funds for UNICEF (just as Samuel and Rhoda gathered pennies for Palestine), they bake cookies to raise funds for the Cambodians. They have been given feminist literature and subjected to my running debunking comments on the sex roles in popular TV comedies. They are concerned with problems of energy, ecology, race relations. In part due to the Vietnam War they consider themselves as nationless, as unattached souls, as involved in the drama of South America as in the injustices in South Africa. Unlike the Greenberg children, they do not feel a particular pull toward one group or another and have taken part in no pro-Soviet Jewry demonstrations. They are, however, not strangers in America. They don't expect, as my parents might have, to be excluded from certain schools, resorts or housing districts. They have never directly or indirectly experienced anti-Semitism. They share with me certain empty spaces where a sense of who they are and who they were and where they came from is thin, slippery and just possibly inadequate.

Statistics are uncertain, but approximately thirty-five percent of young Jewish people may be intermarrying. The attendance at synagogues steadily declines except for a small group of returnees, of people becoming more traditional, of student radicals finding new outlets for their idealism, their absolutism, in fanatic, mystical Chasidic movements. Judaism and Jewishness in America (with some exceptions) appear to be thinning. (Along with the loss of Yiddish comes a loss of the Jewish ethnicity.) The parade narrows at its front end.

Wait, this may be only appearance, a temporary direction of history. There are pulls, strong pulls, in the opposite direction, pulls that mandate a return to Jewishness, to acceptance of oneself as a Jew. There are strong forces at work within the Jewish community working for a better role for women within the Jewish framework. If they are successful they will make it possible for many daughters and sisters to remain and return. There is perhaps a Hegelian dialectic at work where universalism stretched to its utmost will snap and rebound into its opposite and the nation will find itself welcoming back its prodigal sons and daughters. Perhaps these beshoeth (returnees) will join the waves of fundamentalism that are now giving us born-again presidents, Yankee stadiums filled with Jehovah's Witnesses and Jesus demonstrations that stretch miles down Massachusetts Avenue.

Professor Cuddihy (a sociologist at Hunter College), in his book *The Ordeal of Civility* (New York: Basic Books, 1974), defines modernization as refinement. Talcott Parsons (the famous sociologist) says that modernization, the process released by the Industrial Revolution, the French and American revolutions, creating the Protestant ethic, the forms of capitalism, required a continuing differentiation. Cuddihy describes it this way: "Differentiation is the cutting edge of the modernization process, sundering cruelly what tradition has joined. It splits ownership from control, it separates church from state (the Catholic drama), ethnicity from religion (the Jewish drama), nuclear from extended families, it frees poetry from painting and painting from representation." If this definition is accurate, it is clear that Judaism, an inclusive condition, Yiddishkeit, a life with people, sharing the same group memories, repeating the same rituals for thousands of years, depending on the unchanging circular nature of religious time, is unsuited for modernization, for a world where most people are strangers and hanging on to ancient ways excludes you from the mainstream.

But after the Holocaust how can anyone feel that modernization is altogether a good thing? How can one admire technique severed from morality? Differentiation, higher technologies, more isolation of the self, the splitting and splitting of everything including atoms, can no longer be regarded as a benign historical process. The fact of the Holocaust, its massiveness, its irrational terror, its reduction of human life to excrement, calls into question the validity, the viability, of this very Western civilization we were rushing head over heels to join. With just a blink of an eye, a subtle shift of the mind, and the parade of assimilating Jews becomes the line on the railroad stations of Treblinka and Auschwitz. Questions of manners, civility, etiquette, accent, emancipation, education, universality versus tribalism are all wiped out in the crematoria. In a stroke we are back to less civilized times when there were no shades of complicating gray.

The Cuddihy book states that the Jew made a scene in the Diaspora because of his medieval lack of etiquette or misunderstanding of the Protestant ethic, his lack of experience in the difference between public and private places. This reduces the impending tragedy and tragedies that had been to matters of style and form. While those may certainly have their place on a sociologist's operating table, like cosmetic surgery, they should move over for cancer patients, appendectomies and the other stuff of life and death. When Cuddihy, tracing the origin of Freud's discovery of the Oedipal complex itself, makes a huge issue of Freud's shame at his father's unheroic response to the Gentile who knocked his new fur hat into the gutter, it seems quite obvious that the incivility, the scene, the transgression against "niceness," the Jewish or Gentile kind, is made by the attacker, the goy. The Oedipus complex deals with violence of lust, of primitive childhood sexual feelings and the fears and guilts these evoke. The universality of the id (which is not, as Cuddihy would have it, the Yid) is the untempered human impulse for devouring, self-centered aggression. It is not the Jew whose id is out of control, but the Gentile neighbor's who carries incivility to the edge of murder and beyond. The "Yid" in fact was among the most controlled of humankind; regulations existed that modulated the free flow of all his appetites, sexual, oral and other.

It is true that as assimilating Jews we were implicitly encouraged to ape the manners and style of the Gentile world. It was in the service of moving up that my mother would have greatly appreciated it if I had seen my way clear to falling in love with a Loeb, a Warburg or a Schiff. These families were closer to Gentile (less Jewish). However, these matters of form were not matters of true civility, not matters of true tact, true consideration, true politeness, reserve or anything of the kind. They were only the fashion of the ruling class, nothing less and nothing more, and when one thinks of the barbarism that lies just beneath those manners, I am ashamed that I permitted myself to be shaped and molded by them in any way at all. Abbie Hoffman, of sixties fame, who believed in the healing power of vulgarity, had a certain point. I was taught to say thank you and please by a Bavarian nurse whose culture in retrospect seems crude.

My distance from Yiddishkeit makes possible progression up the social ladder in America, but it in no way signifies a movement toward a superior culture. The graceless, loud, emotional, wrong-accented, wrong-languaged ones, whose dress was odd, did not make or cause the major scene in the Diaspora; that was left to the heirs of the Protestant ethic, the Krupps and the Farbens, the Eichmanns. It was left for the Catholic pope to hide Fascist war criminals and for the Catholic convents to turn away Jewish refugees. It was the Polish lumpenproletariat who broke into the ghetto and attacked the Jews in the streets as German planes flew over Warsaw. Whose etiquette was that? It was the French middle class who cooperated with the Germans in deporting trainloads of Jewish children to their death. So if Sartre talks about the assimilated Jews as nonauthentic men, one wonders what he would have to say about the authenticity of the bourgeois Frenchman who was able to reconcile the teachings of Jesus with the political expediency of the moment. That Frenchman may have been born knowing his La Fontaine, his Descartes, his manners may have been superb and natural, but his civility, his level of civilization, was in question.

The implications of the Holocaust for Judaism are multiple and seem to pull in two opposing directions. If we consider Judaism as a religion, the first great religion in the world, the monotheistic vision of Moses on Sinai, it would seem that the experience of the camps broke (in Rabbi Greenberg's words) the covenant God had made with the Jews. The concept of the Chosen People becomes in the showers of Auschwitz a grim Jewish joke, a piece of black humor. Piety cannot survive, transformed into satire or irony. It is an obscenity, as Rabbi Greenberg writes, to imply that the children who were tossed into the burning ovens died for some sin of their own ritual omissions, some impurity of their young souls. It is impossible for many of us to accept the Kiddush Hashem. Because of the technological capacities of the Nazi and the vastness of the devastation he caused, it seems absurd to conceive of God's participation or presence in the world of the camps or the trains. To think of God as the master of cruelty is to take the first and irrevocable step in denying His existence. If God was silent, as some say, that too is without excuse. If God had some plan in His mind that required the Holocaust to take place, such as warning the world of the evils to come, that betrays an incredible disregard for human life. It shows more sadism than is tolerable in a God, even in a God invented and designed by man. If the event of the Holocaust is to the Jews as the Crucifixion is to the Gentiles, then it is a cross too many had to bear. It is a Good Friday without an Easter Sunday. It makes a mockery of man's prayers, and the Jew with his t'fillin and his tallis cuts a ridiculous figure, not because he isn't stylish in the galut but because his God has forsaken him and he refuses to admit it.

The Jews, of course, have gone on believing and worshiping their God through two thousand years of disaster. They did not give up with the destruction of the First Temple and the exodus to Babylonia. They tolerated the destruction of the Second Temple and they developed ways to codify, to continue, to preserve, teach and retain God's laws through centuries of inquisitions, pogroms, forced migrations, forced conversions, martyrdoms to Catholics, Protestants, Turks, Syrians, Russians, Poles, French and, of course, Germans. But after the Enlightenment had arrived, the breaking down of the ghetto walls began, all the world was reaping the fruits of the Renaissance, of the new sciences, of the humanities, it was thought anti-Semitism would die. But again in the flowering of civilization, the monster of violent prejudice re-appears and that is too much to bear. This God cannot be loved, and fearing Him doesn't help either. For many of us the Holocaust marks the end of the religion, but paradoxically enough the Holocaust simultaneously marks the point of reconnection of this modern assimilated Jew to Jewishness, to tradition, to history, to bloodlines. The Holocaust (not because it dragged in the assimilated society along with the rest) forces a moral choice.

I was discussing with a friend, a Gentile, gentle psychiatrist of good breeding and goodwill, William Styron's book *Sophie's Choice.* The book tells the story of a Polish woman who survives the camps only to die at the hands of a Jewish madman in Brooklyn. I try to explain why I feel the book is so subtly anti-Semitic, why it offends me. The animus of the work seems directed at the Jewish literary establishment that Styron fears may steal his limelight or not allow him a piece of the pie. The Poles certainly suffered from the Nazis, but not systematically, not men, women and children, without possibility of disguise or escape, treated like vermin or lice. The Poles themselves were so anti-Semitic that they made it possible for Hitler to move against the Jews. In Styron's book the Jews of Europe are a faceless mass, while every aspect of his Polish heroine's feelings is explored. The Jews in America are pictured as small-minded, petty, materialistic, as cock-teasers, bureaucrats or madmen. The sole exception is the urologist brother whose role is no more than that of the stereo-typical Jewish doctor. (Even anti-Semites may one day need a Jewish doctor.) The book is structured with the double plot of Stingo's need to lose his virginity, particularly with Sophie, and our need to know Sophie's full story, the center of her tragedy. The book climaxes (forgive the pun) with Stingo's intercourse with Sophie and her telling him the story of her horrific choice of which child to save from the gas chambers. There is something artistically and morally wrong in this con-juncture of themes.

As I talk I find I am trembling; my hand is shaking notice-ably.

My kind friend is looking at me, puzzled. "You certainly feel strongly about it, don't you?"

I nod. I realized that we had different histories, different identifications, and my efforts to explain were becoming less clear the harder I tried. He sees the Holocaust as another ex-ample of the problem of evil in the world. I am personally con-nected to it. "There but for the grace" is part of it, I suppose, but beyond that there is a bonding, a coupling, a connection with the victims that is as deep as my genes. One kind of Jew-ishness is that forged in opposition to the savagery and bru-tality of others. This Jewishness is not mere masochistic victim identification, it is a positive determination to rage against, to fight the oppressor. Deborah Greenberg said, "I will fight all my life to make sure it will never happen again." It is hard to explain to someone who doesn't feel it and it forms an irreducible bond, a tie, among all those who do.

Rabbi Greenberg conceives of a time when Jews will include the Holocaust in their traditional ceremonies, when the exodus from Egypt and the story of the slavery under the pharaoh will be joined in ceremonial weight and remembrances of the Holocaust. The problem with this connection is that one wonders why God saved the Jews in Egypt only to bury so many of them in Europe. It is hard to conceive of the Holocaust being connected to any occasion which thanks or honors God, but perhaps?

Non-Jews are also appalled at the extermination camps, but they respond as universalists. They see man's savagery erupting once again and breaking the terms of the social contract. They place the blame on human nature, perhaps on Freud's prematurely discredited death wish, on the sadism and the rage, the murderous aggression of humankind which in turn eluded controls and found political expression in the Nazi party that became a royal highway for a faceless barbarism. The religious Gentile sees the Holocaust as an example of man's fall from grace, an example of original sin, or the problem of evil in God's universe. He does whatever theological maneuvers are comfortable for him to broaden the murder of the Jews into the arena of evil itself. There he is more at home. He has learned to live with the serpent in the garden if not the results of tribalism itself. The Gentile goes on from the Holocaust to discuss My Lai, Hiroshima, Cambodia, and at a safe emotional distance from the events of all these catastrophes, he sees global implications, makes connections between Palestinians and Pakistanis, Biafrans and Cubans. For the Jew the matter is considerably less cerebral, less global and more passionate. I believe in 1980 that the Nazi could reappear at my children's door; the threat is personal.

Freud, writing in *The Future of an Illusion*, confesses that he cannot easily understand mysticism because he had not had any personal mystical experiences. He believes that the "oceanic merging with the galaxies" sentiments that have been described to him may be remnants in later life of sensations of the infant at the mother's breast and the mystical yearning involved by that searching for a recreation of that early oneness, that symbiotic union of infant well-being in the folds of the mother's body. This seems reasonable. I too have never had any mystical experiences. Even in adolescence, when they are likely to occur, the self-consciousness of my mind, endlessly translating experience into words and evaluating and reevaluating those words, excluded me from those sensations of harmony, the all in one and one in all, the unity with God that I have read about.

I have, however, one mystical spot that this examination of Jewish assimilation has brought out. To feel identified with a group of nonblood relatives, to separate out their destiny as particularly involving yours, to relate to their narrow escapes from extermination, to rejoice in the Warsaw resistance, to rejoice with the Israelis at Entebbe, to feel some part of oneself invested in the historical line; which means you are not only connected to other living people who are most likely most unlike you, but as well you are connected to the legions of the dead who are certainly unlike you by any rational standards; to relate oneself as a member of a group that includes Biblical characters, Yemenites, Russians, Chasidim, as well as Reform Jews in Shaker Heights is only explicable by admitting to a mystical, suprarational connection. The minute you say your body is a part of others' bodies you are in the realm of historical romance, mystical belief. Freud, who struggled with his Judaism, had this mystical belief too. In a speech to B'nai B'rith in 1926, he said:

That you were Jews could only be agreeable to me; for I was myself a Jew, and it had always seemed to me not only unworthy but positively senseless to deny the fact. What bound me to Jewry was (I am ashamed to admit) neither faith nor national pride, for I have always been an unbeliever and was brought up without any religion though not without a respect for what are called the "ethical" standards of human civilization. When I felt an inclination to national enthusiasm I strove to suppress it as being harmful and wrong, alarmed by the warning examples of the peoples among whom we Jews live. But plenty of other things remained over to make the attraction of Jewry and Jews irresistible—many obscure emotional forces, which were the more powerful the less they could be expressed in words, as well as a clear consciousness of inner identity, the safe privacy of a common mental construction. And beyond this there was a perception that it was to my Jewish nature alone that I owed two characteristics that had become indispensable to me in the difficult course of my life. Because I was a Jew I found myself free from many prejudices which restricted others in the use of their intellect; and as a Jew I was prepared to join the Opposition and to do without agreement with the "compact majority."

I had thought I had escaped this connection, that like the wicked child I had asserted my ego as separate from the forced march of Jewish history. I had thought that since I had removed God from my life, the thin, watered-down Jewishness I had learned as a child would wither and disappear.

"Remember the days of old, consider the ages past, ask your father he will inform you, your elders will tell you" (Deut. 32:7).

I had thought I had cut out the roots of the tree that was causing too much shade in my garden, that was taking up too much room and embarrassed me with its old gnarled limbs and prevented me from planting new varieties of colorful and exotic plants from far-off places. The tree without its roots has surprised me with its staying power.

I am walking in the Connecticut woods near the Shepaug River. A rainstorm has just passed and the leaves are dark and moist and the ground is pungent. Dr. Leonard Weinroth, a psychiatrist, a man well in his sixties, tells me that once years ago he had planned to write a study of Jewry after Sabbatai Zevi. He had a theory that the Chasidic movement came about as the Jews in their disappointment at their false messiah were regressing in their religious forms to kinds of hysterical and childlike religious practices. He wanted to write about this aspect of Jewish history with a psychiatrist's perspective. But the time didn't come. He was only an amateur historian.

"It's too late for me now," he says.

"Are you religious?" I ask.

"Of course not," he answers. "I am a cultural Jew, a secular Jew. I am interested in everything Jewish except God."

"And your son?" I ask.

"He has some Jewish identity. It's not crucial to me if it dies out. I have no fierce interest in the Jewish future. If my grandchildren are not Jewish, so what?"

For years we have been arguing and teasing each other at dinner parties, he thinking I am a Jewish renegade and I thinking he is a narrow chauvinist, and suddenly the situation reverses itself. I care that the Jewishness continues. I am saddened at the thought of an end. The tradition has been too rich, too full, too poignant, too ripe with human effort just to dwindle off. Of course it matters. The Holocaust makes it matter. But how does a cultural Jew assure continuation? Without the forms of the religion the culture grows thinner with each generation. An insoluble problem? Perhaps. I listen to the sounds of the river. The rain returns with increased density and hits against the rocks with determination. I can't see the river's beginning or end.

It is true that of the thirteen articles of faith of Maimonides I cannot "in perfect faith" or even in imperfect faith believe a single one of them. I have read them many times. I have tried to pretend to myself that I could accept the first one.

"I believe with the perfect faith that the Creator, blessed be His name, is the author and guide of everything He has created and that He alone has made, does make and will make all things."

I have tried substituting other words like space, nature, spirit. If faith is a great Kierkegaardian leap across the abyss of doubt, of rationality, I am left on the wrong side of the divide. I shiver at the eleventh article of faith from Maimonides' commentary on the Mishnah:

"I believe with perfect faith that the Creator, blessed be His name, rewards those who keep His commandments and punishes those who transgress His commandments." This one is like pouring salt into an open wound. Impossible.

Lewis Thomas in *Lives of a Cell* discusses the idea that bees may in fact not be single organisms but parts of one larger life-form. Ants, termites, parasites, bacteria and other insects or animals whose life cannot be sustained separate from the community matrix may be one body, misunderstood by scientists all these years. Perhaps this odd mystical connection to the Jewish peoplehood is like this too. We only appear as separate organisms but in some profound way are a unified though diversified entity. In humans, of course, the life of this mystical organism depends on education. You have to be indoctrinated to be a member, otherwise there is no bond. This indoctrination has to be continually shored up by the repetitions of taboos such as those against intermarriage, eating nonkosher food, and so forth. The fact that the Jew can survive outside the tribe makes us different from the bee, whose organic life ends if it is separated from its shelter. On the other hand, one's life as a Jew also ends if separated from the others, if not for the Jew himself then for his children and grandchildren. If a Jew breaks the taboo and leaps the ghetto walls and pulls himself out of the tradition, a tradition that functions like the bee's hive to make a unity that is more than the sum of its parts, he must deny a part of himself—the mystical part—developed perhaps like hand skills in early childhood but still a part of the self that both belongs to and is the tribe represented in the self.

Terrence Des Pres, in his book *The Survivor*, suggests that cooperation, giving acts, caring for another, are part of our genetic survival makeup, or our humanness itself: "There was an instinctive depth to the emergence of social order through help and sharing. Human interchange goes on all the time everywhere. But in concentration camps it was more naked, more urgently pursued. Judging from the experience of survivors, 'gift morality' and a will to communion are constitutive elements of humanness." If this is true, it may also be true that the tribal nature of the Jewish experience is biologically as well as mystically experienced.

Having reasserted connection to the tribe in grand terms, I immediately feel claustrophobic and this claustrophobia cannot be hidden or denied. Having received a secular education, without the reinforcing Hebrew learning of the Solomans' Herzlia, having lived outside the ghetto walls, I would not return to a place of such ethnic particularity that I would lose the world at large. My brother once took a trip through Europe as a teenager with a Jewish group on their way to Israel. In their few hours in Paris and Rome they visited the Jewish quarter instead of Notre Dame or the Vatican. My father, who eventually took a Catholic wife, drove through the small towns of Italy looking in the cemeteries for Jewish names that would signify an ancient Jewish presence in the area. No tourist retrieving an amphora from the Mediterranean was as delighted as he when stumbling on a Jewish dead of the fifteenth century. All political acts cannot be judged in terms of whether or not they are good for the Jews, that is, Israel. This promotes a clannishness that is suffocating and possibly dangerous in a world as interlocked, interrelated, economically, socially, politically as ours. The Jews in one small medieval town in Italy celebrated with an annual holiday the putting up of the ghetto walls and gates because they felt that the walls would keep out the taboo Christian and the resulting segregation suited them well. Being walled in, psychologically or literally, is no cause for a holiday. The advantages of a traditional

...ociety over a modern one can best be discussed after a solid worldly education, the proper vaccines, access to decent plumbing and the sensual and intellectual joys of a variety of tastes in food, art, music and philosophy.

I have as well more personal kinds of Jewish claustrophobia. While "life is with people" and shtetl intimacy seem like an antidote to our alienated, lonely, difficult path, nostalgia and sentimentalizing travel in that direction also. It was wonderful for the Soloman clan. But the bonds of family were in many cases suffocating and deadly. Even in my bourgeois scene several of my cousins fell victim to the family's controls. One who wanted to be a history teacher was forced into the shirt business for economic safety and there his soul languished away. Another, although interested in the world of ballet and art, was forced into his family business that interested him not at all. I have female cousins whose mothers told them what to wear well past their fortieth birthday. I have another cousin who was in nursing school in a distant city but gave it up to return to her parents in the Bronx. She lives with them still. She gave up her independence to maintain the "life is with people" of her childhood. Her income, her possibilities for travel, for expansion, were all severely limited by that decision. Too much closeness can be a wicked thing. The strong family judgments about who was suitable to marry and what was proper in dress and life-style were limiting to all my cousins. Fear of what others would say, fear of doing something different, made the Gemeinschaft something less than a total blessing. Dividing everything in the world into goyish or Jewish (translate forbidden or acceptable) is a sign of being further back on the assimilation parade than I could ever take myself. This description of limiting clannishness applies not just to Jews but to all immigrant groups in America and is a reflection of class and economic conditions rather than religious ones.

Blu Greenberg speaks of the importance of family in Jewish traditions. I worry about this. All groups are concerned with family, and close and loyal families are part of the por-

traits of all ethnic traditional styles. Jews are not the only ones
to discover the virtues of this support system, and Gentiles of
all kinds too take care of their little children and watch over
their old people (before the modern world interrupts their
traditional ways). But it is true that Blu Greenberg's family
has a special radiance, a cohesion and a beauty that come from
the Jewishness at the center that draws all parts together and
holds them in a strongly felt unity. I cannot talk myself out
of admiring her family and the Soloman family. My life would
have been happier, my portion of human contentment larger,
if I had been one of them. But what might have been is of no
interest. Today I feel a renewed or new connection to Jewishness, an amazed connection that supersedes all my ambivalences and doubts.

Freud's explanation of mystical feelings as originating in
infancy could explain the connection of self to tribe, a natural
extension of that early feeling of connection to the caretakers,
the parents or others who provide life sustenance. Perhaps humans cannot go from the tight connection of the mother and
child to a free floating about in the large universe. The Yiddish
language has been called the mama-loshen (mother tongue).
The group that extends out into the future and back into our
past may psychologically form the bridge to the outer world,
to the world of our children and our ancestors. My sense of
belonging to a Jewish nation, resting as it does on neither religion nor learning, may be no more than a kind of wholeness
hunger, a sometime desire to do away with the fragmentation
of the modern. It may also be a disguised, unconscious crav-
ing for immortality. (The Messiah coming one day and bringing resurrection to the whole body of worthy dead seems like a
medieval fairy tale conceived not so much out of piety, but
out of that all-too-human need to deny death and assert permanence of self.) The tribal nature of the Jewish experience
without the apocalyptic end grants a kind of immortality to its
members. The intensity of feeling of belonging to a particular
past and a special future, to the lines of generations that have

celebrated, prayed, remembered the same things, used the same language, this does grant a form of egoless immortality. The particular self will die but the Jewish self will live on.

I question whether this Jewishness of mine is mere masochistic identification with the victim. Jewish history has some heroic tales to tell, the Maccabees, Judith, Esther and Joshua and David, Samson and Saul, but it is also filled with endless tales of suffering, and the more modern history becomes the more ghastly the stories and the more vivid the details. The Book of Job is just a prelude to other tales of blood-letting and plague-inspired massacres. The autos-da-fé recounted are endless. Cuddihy calls this the lachrymose history of the Jews and suggests its use was to excuse the backward condition, that is, nonmodern, of the Ostjude. Maybe so, but it was also accurate. Its effect on a child is painful. It appears the world is divided into good and bad, goy and Jew, and it is the goy who harms the Jew, not the other way around (at least until Rabbi Kahane and the West Bank). Moral decency, sympathy for the victim, sympathy for those who suffer, these are building blocks of the mystical connection to Judaism. It seems not so much to be a matter of indulging in masochism as to be a matter of aligning oneself with innocence. In Christianity, Christ suffers for everyone. In Judaism, everyone suffers and it is not quite clear who for. It cannot be denied that suffering is one of the chief glues of group unity. It works.

Israel has been long believed to symbolize the end of Jewish suffering. Many people, among them Rabbi Greenberg, see Israel as the redemption of the Holocaust, the Easter Sunday we have been lacking. The State of Israel, the return of the people to Zion, partially undoes the demoralization of the Holocaust experience.

Political Zionism ended with the Jews taking into their own hands the destiny of this despised and troubled people. The hope was that in forming a nation, in making Jews normal, protecting them from the political disruptions, the waves of anti-Semitism of the West, the galut would end, the Diaspora would finish and next year in Zion would find an improved, strengthened, confident Jewry, able once again to bring down its enemies and hold up its head in national pride.

Anna Ornstein says that nothing destroys her more than a threat to Israel's safety. I too feel that Israel, a political entity, with brave soldiers and terrible bombs, marks a necessary turning point in Jewish destiny. It is possible to be connected to the events in Israel without ever having set foot on the soil or having made plans to move. That is one of the contradictions and complications of being Jewish. In the Ukraine, the Jews buried their shrouded dead with twigs between their fingers so that they might dig their way straight through the earth to Palestine when the Messiah came. There had always been the possibility of being physically in one nation while psychologically within another. Now a third level is added, the actual commitment to a second actual nation that functions as a symbol of Jewish vindication, Jewish survival. It sits precariously in the Mideast, a monument itself to the dead of Dachau, a sign that survival is after all possible.

There is, of course, nothing simple in the Jewish condition. Even now the actual Israel itself becomes dubious as the place of redemption. Hannah Arendt, who was a Zionist but did not believe in a political state, said in 1937 that if the Jews turned the Palestinians into a refugee population, it would awaken their nationalism and that the Jews would find themselves surrounded by millions of hostile Arabs and would be forced to turn to one of the two major world powers for military assistance. She predicted that the Jews would become an embattled and militaristic society, denying in the process the very essence of the ethical, moral Judaism that had managed to survive through so many centuries of repression. Hannah Arendt in the thirties was afraid that such a Jewish state would be sacrificed in some balance-of-power struggle and the resulting disaster would be a blow of such immense proportion that Judaism might never recover and its long history end. Her premature concerns have the frightening ring of prophecy about them today. Those Jews who only want Israel to exist after the arrival of the Messiah may have their way. For the rest of us the fragility of Israel remains a grief, a personal vulnerability, a fear that is constant and insistent.

We are sitting around the table after dinner. The crickets are making their summer sounds. The raccoons are waiting to attack the garbage. A psychoanalyst friend, lights his cigar.

"It's the same anti-Semitism that's always been. Only now it has the excuse of being anti-Israel. The entire world is against us. It always has been and it always will be. You want the Jews to be nice and quiet. They'll hate us for that, too."

"No," I begin to protest, to argue, but his bitterness touches mine and in solidarity we look out into the Connecticut night and together feel angry and afraid. But I remember the strange sounds on the roof of the synagogue in Metz that Gluckel described, and how the women in the balcony panicked and six were trampled to death or suffocated in the stampede. It's important as we think about Israel not to hear noises on the roof that are not there and hasten our own destruction.

And yet, a part of the self that is not tribal, that is leftish, literary, feels a need to identify also with the Palestinians, with their life in camps (never mind who prolonged it and why), their legitimate nationalism; their hurt pride is a painful consideration also. Having been betrayed so often, the Jew may now be betrayed by his own lack of trust, his unwillingness to compromise.

This connection of mine to Israel is sentimental, unearned by personal sacrifice or physical commitment. It is Holocaust-related in its passion and is finally part of the fantasy life, the part played in political activity where Davids and Goliaths, Saint Georges and dragons tilt at each other eternally.

If Israel fails, if there is another Diaspora, I suppose the Jewish history books will simply get longer and longer and the words "Next year in Jerusalem" will grow in poignancy until they break in pieces like matzoh crumbs on the table. I suppose I wish that my family had moved to Israel in 1948. (My mother would never have moved away from her sisters and brothers into a situation where she would have to cook or clean. She was not a pioneer.) I think that had we moved during my childhood the discomforts of the language change would have been quickly outweighed by the advantages of living in a place with a national purpose, with clear enemies, with defined borders. There was something left to conquer, it was a place small enough so that the contributions of a particular soul might have mattered. If only when I reached the proper age I had been less of a princess and more of an adventurer, but the ifs of one's past must be discarded; as in wearing a hair shirt, the resulting melancholy becomes self-indulgent. The very comforts of my childhood had created certain traps. I had an imagination that could cross an ocean, I had a mouth that could say anything, but my body could not wander too far from my mother's.

Herzl thought that all Christians were either overt or covert anti-Semites. He had heard them scream at the Dreyfus trial, "Mort aux juifs." He heard it correctly, history has proved. Assimilation is an attempt on the part of those of us who live it to cover our eyes. Perhaps in America, Jewish destiny will be different. In America for the first time Jews are living in a country where there are populations more despised than they. In America there are traditions of interfaith respect. There is a Constitution that appears permanent or at least can fool a lot of people into thinking it is. In America Jews have been free to exploit poorer, more ignorant people who have been excluded longer from the fruits of modernity. It seems at best a Pyrrhic victory.

My stepdaughter, who speaks a fluent French, spent part of her junior year in Paris. She returned talking about wanting to live there permanently, to reimmigrate to the continent of family origin. She saw Paris as beautiful, cosmopolitan, exciting. It would be hard to have her live so far away but after all we believe in each generation's finding its own way, moving on from the past, seizing its opportunity. She has every right to move as far from her father as he moved from his. If it made her happy that would be sufficient for us. There are unwritten laws on the parade of assimilation. But I had a further anxiety. I thought of Dreyfus, and of Sartre's eloquent description of anti-Semitism in France. I thought of the gare Montparnasse filled with Jewish children, frightened, hungry, waiting to be slaughtered. How could she live there? I wondered. How can a Jew walk those streets without remembering? My grandparents, her grandparents, had escaped Europe in time to save their lives to ensure that their genes would continue. And now this beautiful child with her luminous eyes and her classic Semitic face, her fierce intelligence, her appetite for everything, wants to return. I think perhaps it is unfair for one generation to impose its nightmares on another.

There will always be isolated events, synagogues defaced and crosses burned, but it is hard to imagine these fevers of hate lighting up cataclysmic fires in which we will all be consumed. I do not think that if Israel were abandoned by a future president that the people of this country would take to butchering in their Jewish suburbs at Eastertide. It seems the stuff of CIA thrillers written for twelve-year-olds to propose that a president might round up Jews to silence them about his Mideast policy. History cannot be counted on to repeat itself and the revival of National Socialism in this country seems unlikely. The very flaws of American society, its homogenized bland materialism, the lack of drama. Its sentimentality, its therapeutic "me" orientation, all protect against the reemergence of a virulent anti-Semitism.

Jews in this country look and act like everyone else (small exceptions made for the folk in the mitzvah mobile) and they share the vulgarity, the game-show mentality of the others. There is little to single them out. I know German Jews blended in too and that the assimilated went to the ovens with the others, but this country constitutes itself by absorbing multiple nations. In one sense it is a large refugee camp and it. is to everyone's advantage to say polite things about the others or most of the others. Jews might have been saved had there been blacks, Puerto Ricans and Mexicans in Europe. I don't think the Jewish nation will flourish here in reaction to persecution. If assimilation doesn't end the Jewishness of many families it will be because of positive, innovative happenings generated by Jews themselves. It will be because Jewishness will prove itself capable of sifting through old cultures and making itself necessary. Judaism has, after all, survived the threat of Hellenism, Christianity, why not modernism too?

Now let's look at the religion itself that has so warmly sustained Samuel and Rhoda Soloman and Blu and Irving Greenberg and their children and the millions of other American Jews who are active in their synagogues, who keep many of the 613 laws of observance. The religion is structured on two major lines that of course overlap and interweave. The first is ritual and prayer and the second is remembering, recounting the shared history. The rituals that deal with the reading of the Torah, the saying of the daily prayers, renewing the relationship of man to God, are only compelling if one has a pious nature and is a believer. If the faith is not there the ritual is empty and tedious.

Many Jewish rituals have to do with the care of the home, the keeping of kashruth and the ritual cleansing of women after menstruation, as well as honoring the Sabbath. In anthropology, Claude Lévi-Strauss and friends have shown us that all tribal structures derive from the need to create a pure and an impure and to distinguish between them. The kashruth is no exception. By the light of modern social science we can see it as the human primitive need to ritualize inner and outer, to tame the cannibal impulse and to subject those impulses to rule and order. The more precise the laws, the more chaotic the impulses that needed to be brought under some civilizing force. The division of food into meat and milk, says Rhoda Soloman, is our way of letting God's law constantly into our lives.

Education in the social sciences leads to universalism by

emphasizing the common human underpinnings of forms of religious and social organization. This universalism simultaneously enlightens while robbing of the particular significance of one's own way of doing things. The concept of the impurity as coming from without does not sit too well with all we know of man's unconscious fantasy life. We can't help noticing the universality of such images as burning bushes and magical wine cups. Universality that comes from observing unities of human behavior, while making one more modern, more part of a differentiated split world, also paradoxically makes one more of a general human being. When allegiances break, a thinning of connections follows.

Ritual controls, like the Jewish laws that determine Jewish sexual behavior, are not so much concerned with right and wrong as with impulse and containment. The Episcopalian priest Father Nargesian explained church ritual this way: "You kiss the baby because you love it and you love the baby because you kiss it." By this circle you love God because you perform the rituals and you perform the rituals in order to love God. Demands, enormous, difficult, real demands, are part of all religions that have kept their adherents for more than a second of historical time. But when one realizes that these rituals are elaborations of similar human means of coping throughout the ages around the globe, and that they have unconscious roots in primitive conditions, it is hard to take them with absolute seriousness. It is hard not to drift away.

In Judaism the large body of ritual law leads to internecine quarreling; just which laws do you obey? How faithfully do you obey them? And each group feels itself holier than the others and there is so much internal criticism and contempt for one practitioner over the other. The arguments over the distinctions of who is a good Jew and who is a bad Jew and whether one's neighbor warmed her food on the Sabbath or didn't and whether it is or is not all right to drive to the hospital on a High Holiday, these discussions bring on acute claustrophobia.

I respect the Judaic law many Jews choose to live under, all varieties of it. Perhaps had I been brought up with those laws I might have continued to practice them even when I felt them not to be of divine origin but expressions of universal human responses. I might have found them as enriching, comforting and supportive as do the Solomans. I can see that these ritual laws do seem to tame the savage within and give the sense of placating the savage without. They are intimations of the divine in daily life, or so they seem to believers.

I do find somewhat strange this constant referring back to the wisdom of rabbis whose bones turned to ash many centuries ago. It seems like a disguised form of ancestor worship, and worshiping an ancestor instead of an idol seems only a matter of taste and not a sign of abstract thought or conceptual gift. Here I admit I have never liked anyone else's rules and I am forever puttering around at the edges of taboos wherever I find them. Many people will see this as a character failing. They may be right.

I admire the Solomans for their real goodness, for their wholeness. I love them for the integrity of their lives and the sweetness and courageousness of their spirit. If it were not such a soul violation of who I am and what I have become, I might leave my spot in the assimilation parade and join them. I cannot. I cannot (even as I wish it) become a traditional Jew. This would be a nonauthentic position. Such a conversion would be imposing a layer of strange forms on an alien spirit. I would then really be a parvenue, a nouveau, a ridiculous person, like the Jewish opportunist who converts to Christianity. I would violate myself in making such a return.

Naturally the matter of prayers is difficult for a person of little faith. The content of the prayers seems to be in the form of thanks, begging, wooing and humbling oneself before the Almighty. At Channukah the candles are lit to commemorate the miracle of the saving of the country from the Syrians. It is a holiday that reminds the Jews of a heroic moment when their bravest soldiers were triumphant. The Maccabees have

won and the little bit of oil burns for eight days, a miraculous
gift from God. I would be happier if God had not brought the
Syrians to the doorstep in the first place. I would be more willing to mark the holiday if God did not let innocents die on
all sides in the warfare. It seems just possible that the Jews
have celebrated God for giving too little. Knowing what lies
ahead for the Chosen People makes of this little bit of magic
oil a meager gift indeed. Jews have accepted small miracles
long enough.

The other main pillar of the Jewish religion is remembering.
It is the telling and retelling each year of stories of the past.
The history of the Jews is kept alive in its religious forms, the
exodus from Egypt, the stay in Babylon, the giving of the commandments at Sinai, the destruction of the temples. Jewish religious schools all teach Jewish history and in doing so create
Jewish nationhood. Jewish children know the story of the
Spanish Inquisition and the condition of the Jews in modern
Russia. Jewish schools tell the tale of the sufferings of the
Wandering Jew, who is wandering according to Christian myth
because he mocked Christ and according to the historical fact
because Christians have not truly accepted the teachings of
their Christ. "Remember this," "Remember that." The past is
a part of every Jewish child's experience, not just the holidays
but all through the year, "It is done as it was done," and "It is
said as it was said." Jewish secular law and Jewish religious practices are all based on referrals back to tractates and commentaries of other centuries. This makes Jews continually the witnesses of their own past and gives the odd flavor to their rea-
sonings, as if history were happening in both the vertical and
the horizontal time line, as if things moved forward and stayed
still at the same time.

I saw an exhibit at the Jewish Museum in New York of
treasures and memorabilia salvaged from the Danzig Jewish community and sent to America just before the synagogue
was burned and the population of Jews was deported. In
the museum I saw wall hangings, Torah covers, silver plates

and goblets of extraordinary beauty and grace. I saw pictures of Jewish Boy Scout troops, of schoolchildren, of the high-school classes, of passports and visas some never got a chance to use, of letters to friends and report cards and photographs of the synagogue as the Nazis were demolishing the remains. I took my daughter Katie with me to the museum.

"Do they have a postcard of the synagogue at Danzig?" she asked. She knows I am very generous about buying postcards in museums.

"Why do you want that?" I ask.

"I want to remember it," she said, "always."

I want to remember it too. The remembering part of the Jewish religion is perhaps what can be teased apart from the theological. This witnessing of the past constitutes the bonds of the tribe. Christians tell one story over and over, birth, Crucifixion and Resurrection, and around it they build their moral teachings. Jews tell many stories with many characters in them, and their stories move forward in time over many centuries. It is strange that the Jewish stories read in a sense like a communal crucifixion stretched out in time with a resurrection, stretched out also, so far out that we have not yet come to it. (Perhaps it was not so strange that Sabbatai Zevi converted under the sultan's pressure. He had a need to believe that the Messiah had arrived. If it was not himself he must have assumed it to be the other one.)

After prayer and remembering, the third part of the Jewish experience is language. The Hebrew sounds and the Hebrew rhythmic pattern seem special, mysterious and of a great and ancient beauty. Now perhaps I am romanticizing. When in Israel the housewife calls the plumber and complains of a stoppage, I suppose Hebrew is as plain as any other language. But when in America people say, "In Hebrew we say," and then they say it and then translate it, I think there is a grandeur in it that stems from its age and its sacred uses and the special feeling the speaker has toward the language that was learned and associated with the out of the ordinary in his or her life. It is in part like a child's made-up language, more wonderful because it is private and marks the speaker as a member of a select group. In America, Hebrew sounds profound, sad, magical, like anyone's good mantra, like a terrific jazz solo. Hebrew, like Latin, seems to be truer, purer, because it began closer to the beginnings of things.

The other language of the Jews is Yiddish. Yiddish has been left on the roadside in the assimilation march, abandoned as unnecessary, as too heavy a baggage to carry so far. But the literature, while it has only a brief history, remains. In translation I have read Aleichem, Asch, Singer, the editorials of Abraham Cahan, "The Bintel Brief," and I will forever regret that I can't read them all in the original language. The writers in English whose early language was Yiddish have given me a kind of knowledge of the world I missed. Mike Gold, Henry Roth, Tillie Olsen, Grace Paley, Cynthia Ozick, Bellow, Philip Roth, Malamud, Delmore Schwartz, J. D. Salinger have, together from their different artistic positions (and slightly different positions on the assimilation scale), made a vivid universe of people I might never have known, people who are after all my people even if I didn't know it for a long time.

The Yiddish I don't have (but my brother taught himself to speak and read) seems to me now to carry a culture as complex and crucial as that of the French I labored so hard over in high school. Yiddish-speaking people owned no steel mills and made a very minimal contribution to the gross national product. They were considered uncouth by people whose own manners and mores did not help them live with more wit or soul or taste the fullness of life with any greater style or intensity. It is interesting that the Jewish writers who have come out of the middle classes have not achieved the same level of extraordinary artistry that was reached by those whose childhoods were spent in Yiddish and in more economically uncertain circumstances. I had always thought Yiddish was vulgar. If my mother let a word out of her mouth she wouldn't translate it

for me. The only word I did know had to do with the backside.
I wonder if it wasn't a sign of my own vulgarity to have
thought Yiddish vulgar. It's too late now to mourn the loss.

I wish I had learned Hebrew. I wish it had not been made so
clear that my brother should learn it and that I need not
bother. Now I am always surprised when I hear a woman
speak it. It seems they are doing something remarkable, like
taking engineering courses at MIT or flying a jetliner. It
gives great pleasure to listen to Hebrew, particularly from a
woman.

There are two main taboos laid upon all Jewish people. The
first and most important taboo is not to leave the tribe. The
worst crime against the group is to separate from it, to change
one's name, do one's nose, deny one's link with the others.
The taboo against intermarriage is really only an extension in
practical matters of the first taboo. If you marry a stranger it
will lead to your eventually leaving the tribe, and if you yourself do not, then your children and grandchildren will and so
the body of Jewry will be depleted. Each loss is grieved and
each time someone breaks the taboo the ranks close tighter
behind him. They don't say (not relatives, friends or friends
of relatives) good luck, Godspeed, they vilify and despise.
The family meals in Good as Gold by Joseph Heller are fine
examples of a writer trying to escape. Philip Roth, in his book
The Ghost Writer, needs to bring home a girl of no less Jewishness than Anne Frank in order to mend the fences and regain admission to the Jewish home. At a Jewish wedding you
don't just get married in the eyes of God, you also pledge
yourself to keep a Jewish home (the rabbi adds this Jewish
pledge to the ceremony). In other words, unlike a Gentile
wedding, which is an affair between bride, bridegroom and
Christ, the Jewish wedding is between the young couple, God
and the entire Jewish nation from the ancient patriarchs to
the Israeli Sabras and includes the full range of the Jewish
people in between. A Jewish wedding becomes a tribal rite of
commitment. It is a pledge to the group. No wonder that in

times of affluence Jewish weddings tend to be excessive. One
has to eat, drink and celebrate for the entire nation, not just
for those present in the flesh.

The measure of the attraction out is reflected in the fierce-
ness of the taboo that keeps people in. (That is some kind of
elementary social physics.) There seems to be something in
the imprinting that Jewish children receive that marks them
forever and engages them in a battle with this taboo. ("Before you taught me the difference between night and day, you
taught me goyish and Jewish." Philip Roth in *Portnoy's Complaint*.) When Jews hurl themselves over the taboo, usually
kicking and screaming curses behind them (because like
adolescents they have to fight in order to leave), they can't
help but find themselves filled with ambivalence about their
new place. The nature of a taboo is not to stand aside and let
you pass, but to follow you around for the rest of your days,
calling you names and building fires of regret in your unconscious. The breaking of taboos, or just the thought of breaking
them, has served as the fuel of Jewish literature, Malamud,
Roth, Bellow, Singer, and so forth.

The other major taboo (social, not religious) for the Jewish
nation is against speaking out, informing the goyim, airing
dirty linen. This taboo had its legitimate base in the desire not
to deliver ammunition into the hands of the anti-Semitic
enemy. It was originally not paranoia, it was group protectiveness. The trouble with this taboo is that it crossed, clashed,
with equally strongly felt modern demands on the modern
writer, the artist, the journalist, to tell the truth as one sees it
about one's world, becoming a witness to the universal experience by examining honestly one's own space. This is the basic
animating form of most modern literature, and working in it
meant expressing anger, criticizing at least by implication the
family structure, the particular habits of particular Jewish families who were understood to represent the multitude. This
kind of art requires not literal truth but truth transformed and
recognizable, illuminating. The irony of the modern Jewish

writers is that they could not please both masters at once, and over and over again the necessities of their art became more important than receding group loyalty.

A taboo is simultaneously a barrier and a temptation. As a barrier it increases the level of temptation. I have not fingers and toes enough to count the men I know who can only love the shiksa. They are the ones who have only to look at a Jewish girl and they hear the ghetto gates slamming shut. They may boast about their Jewish wits, they may be pleased that their half-Jewish children are interested in Jewish things, they may crack an unending stream of Jewish jokes in public or private, but they find anti-erotic the familial, the Jewish woman, the woman whose low status is equal to theirs in the eyes of the larger world. They seek the golden-haired, and the tall, to provide for them instant passports to the other side of the tribal walls, away from the mishpocheh (relations, inlaws) to a place where they can breathe freely, away from all the others, a place where they can put down the weight of their history. The dreaded shiksa is not just, as the Freudians would have it, a talisman to protect against incest; she provides the royal road out. Besides, Jewish women are so devalued by the Jewish tradition, they are so traditionally excluded from education and law, that it is no wonder many Jewish men think little of them. The shiksa, while she can't help being female, has not the double stigma of being both female and Jewish.

Ah, this thing about being a Jewish woman, it comes back to me and hurts again. All the world's a patriarchy and Jews in this are no different from anyone else. There are shadings, however, that make it especially uncomfortable to be female and Jewish. The emphasis on tradition, on keeping things the way they were, makes it hard for Jewish women who value their traditions to undo and redo the role they have been assigned. The fact that Jewish communities are more recently arrived from medieval conditions makes the female progress slower. The ghetto, like the rest of the fourteenth-century world, was a place where women were hobbled by law and custom, despised as witches and considered primarily in property terms. In the Enlightenment these attitudes did not disappear but they became more subdued, more indirect.

Jewish women have been excluded from what was long considered the purpose and essence of Jewish life, scholarship and Torah, the perfect study of which was to aid in bringing the Messiah. Though all Christianity also belittles or overidealizes women, Christian females do not suffer the added sting of legal exclusion from the honors of the learned.

"Let the words of the Torah be burned rather than entrusted to women" (Rabbi Eliezer Hyrramus in the Jerusalem Talmud, tractate Sotah, chap. 3, sec. 4).

There has been no easy way for a Jewish woman to distinguish herself (Henrietta Szold aside) in Jewish intellectual work. The practical omission of women from the 613 laws has had the effect of barring women from the center of the religion. It is not simply that they are banished upstairs (that is in itself symbolic but not crucial), it is that they were robbed in the shtetl of Hebrew education, and since education was given the highest of status, what could the female be but the lowest of the low, possibly married to someone of high state?

The laws that surround menstruation and the need for ritual cleansing had the effect of separating the sexes even further by making the woman's biological functions appear impure and unclean, and by implication the woman herself became defiled, not fit for studying next to or for intellectual concerns. It was also assumed that temptation and seduction oozed from her at all times. It was assumed that their bodies were disturbing to God and man except possibly when they were pregnant with sons. Samuel Soloman's brother, also a pediatrician, said to a friend of mine who had just given birth to twin boys and expressed some concern about the double responsibility, "Think how proud you'll be when you walk down the street and show the world you have produced two sons." Alas, if they had been daughters there would have been less cause for rejoicing.

It may have increased the male's desire and sperm flow to have only two weeks a month to enjoy his wife, but it must also have reduced the woman's own sexuality and pleasure in herself to be so untouchable, undesirable, fifty percent of the time. Because the timing of the menstrual restrictions permitted sex just at the woman's ovulation, the tribe may have increased its numbers (and in times when so many children were likely to die this may have had a real meaning), but with all we know of male fear of castration and female sense of having suffered a loss in the assigning of biological gender, it seems a primitive and painful set of laws today.

Women were also feared. Lilith, the Mesopotamian goddess of fertility, was changed in Jewish folklore to the archdemon who might steal your life away while you were sleeping. This fear of women is perhaps the source of the subsequent misogyny. A married woman's hair was cut and she wore the sheitel. It is interesting that when the Nazis were instituting terror in the camps and attempting to annihilate the egos of their victims, they cut their hair; that when the French wished to humiliate women who had cooperated with the Germans, after the war they shaved their heads. Jewish tradition mutilated a young girl's beauty in the name of chastity. Wasn't that also an expression of the community dislike of the female? A sense that she was a mutilated being, not whole? Jews, of course, are a people very concerned with the head, and instead of education the Jewish woman got a wig for her head.

Women in the Christian West were subjected to discrimination, slights against their intelligence and laws against their person and property rights. But women in the shtetl were subjected to all these and certain weighty symbolic laws as well that branded them further as inferior. In the suburbs of America, the Jewish country clubs, in Jewish organizations, the remnants of these stigmata remain. It is hard to hear the world laugh at the Jewish American Princess. It is not her fault if she has been taught that her role in life is to catch a rising man and that she has learned the more money spent on her outsides, the more chance she has for success. Her shallowness is not her cultural error and her future promises to be no laughing matter.

In Francine Klagsbrun's Voices of Wisdom I find this quote from Paula E. Hyman, professor of modern Jewish history at Columbia University: "Within the framework of traditional Judaism women are not independent legal entities, like the minor, the deaf mute and the idiot, they cannot serve as witnesses in a Jewish court. They do not inherit equally with male heirs. They play only a passive role in the Jewish marriage ceremony and they cannot initiate divorce proceedings." The usual rabbinical response to these criticisms is that the woman has the all-important role of care of the family and the home. Gluckel, of course, worked to support her family both while her husband was living and for twenty years afterward. The importance of the home becomes a euphemism for lesser intellectual attainments, for staying in place and not questioning male authority. Certainly women are willing to let men share in the important work of the home in return for sharing the important work of the world.

Cynthia Ozick has written in Lilith, a Jewish feminist magazine: "Item: In the world at large I call myself and am called a Jew. But when on the Sabbath I sit among women in my traditional shul and the rabbi speaks the word 'Jew,' I can be sure that he is not referring to me. For him 'Jew' means male Jew. When my rabbi says 'A Jew is called to the Torah,' he never means me or any other living Jewish woman. My own synagogue is the only place in the world where I, a middle-aged adult, am defined exclusively by my being the female child of my parents. My own synagogue is the only place in the world where I am not a Jew."

There is a certain literalism to Jewish religious customs. If the Lord says to bind words to your forehead that is not taken symbolically as an injunction to repeat them in your mind but literally to bind them there. So the rabbinical misogyny became translated into literal acts against the female body. This literalism makes Jewish feminist work so much more difficult. How odd that a religion that was the very first to conceive of God as an abstract unity should have remained so literal in some areas.

Cynthia Ozick says, "Since Deborah the prophet, we have not had a collective Jewish genius. What we have had is a half-Jewish genius. That is not enough for the people who choose to hear the voice of the Lord of History." It is also degrading and insulting to the female to hear all this: "Remember, son," "Tell your sons," "Ask your father," and this from the words of the Babylonian tractate: "How do women earn merit? By making their children go to synagogue and their husbands to the house of study to learn Mishnah and by waiting for their husbands until they return from the house of study."

In Jewish life it seems that the forces that separate male and female, that mark them as different creatures, that distort the common humanness of both, have won ancient victories; only now, post-Holocaust, with the new threat of assimilation at the doorstep, with the infiltration of ideas from the Socialists, Zionists, the mavericks of the Jewish and non-Jewish world, are there the beginnings of a fight being made to change the status of women within the Jewish religion. The loss of women scholars, the loss of female poets and psalm-makers, of a female Rashi or Maimonides, can never be replaced, but perhaps now at a point when a new covenant can be drawn, as Rabbi Greenberg suggests, women can be given justice. In the same article in *Lilith*, Letty Cottin Pogrebin is quoted as saying, "A life of the Torah is embodied in Hillel's injunction, 'Do not do unto others as you would not have others do unto you.' Men would not like done unto them what is done to women in the name of Halachah."

I wonder if there will be a Judaism or if there is now a Judaism in someone's Reform synagogue or Reconstructionist place that I could take my daughters to without subjecting them to insults. I wonder if the patriarchal tradition would not suffocate the best intentioned of feminist apologias pasted over the top. To be in Judaism is to be in the past as well as the present and the past cannot be rewritten or prettied up to please contemporary views. I wonder if a female Jewish child would not have to take flight from that past just as I did back in the 1940s when our consciousness was lowered deep beneath the synagogue steps and our hopes for ourselves were equally out of reach. I wish I knew how to give back to my mother the dignity she had lost and I wish I knew how to ascertain it, in a Jewish framework, for my daughters. The Greenberg girls, Deborah and Goody, do seem to have a sense of purpose and intellectual strength that might make a Babylonian rabbi quake in his sandals. Deborah's expressed personal ambitions were not equal to her intelligence, but perhaps that's just adolescence. I thought she could easily follow her father into the rabbinate if she chose. They have been raised in a Jewish and feminist household. They have straddled the contradictions and fought some of them out with their brothers and survived. Dr. Soloman is exceedingly of his scholar-daughter. At any rate the contradictions are there and may not be resolved for at least another thousand years.

On the last day of the school year the children attend a lower-school assembly. They are dressed in their good clothes and their hair is washed and braided for the occasion. The parents sit in the balcony and the back rows and the children crane their necks to locate a particular mother and father in the sea of adults behind them. Each class sings a song. There are recorder groups and bells and a lot of shuffling and giggling between the musical numbers. There is a play given by class IV. Then the principal of the school gets up and announces that class I is now class II, and class II is now class III, and all the children stand up very straight and solemnly as this goes on until at last the class IVs take up ribbons and in arches they have formed lead the entire school, singing "Auld Lang Syne," out of the assembly hall.

I know that my nose is turning red and I sniffle and dab at

my eyes with the corner of my sleeve. I am feeling sad that time is passing, that my nine-year-old is now ten, that the grades of school are going by, that the crowd of children before me will be adults in a blink of a historical eyelash. I am feeling fear for all the things that can happen to them in that blink. I am worrying about cancer and accidents and eruptions of despair and growing addictions that may even now be budding in those small bodies. I fear for nuclear disaster and political repression and economic upheaval. I fear what may be done to these children and what they may do to others.

I am sentimental, nostalgic, and I wonder as I hear their excited voices in the hall, what is the matter with me? This is only a lower-school last-day assembly, not a graduation or a wedding or a funeral. Am I mad or do I suffer simply from tradition hunger? I begin to think it really possible that we are animals with an undeniable need for forms to hold and shape our reactions to the passing of time. Without these forms we tend to miss things, to go a bit daft, to get chills in empty hallways. I make so much out of so little out of a need to make much of something. I stop sniffling. I take my daughters home.

Sometimes I feel guilty that after my psychoanalysis I still am searching around for a place to feel comfortable. That I still feel unsatisfied with my particular spiritual arrangements. But after all psychoanalysis is only a therapy. It carries with it a kind of ethos but it is not an ethnicity. It has some heroes and villains, the rudiments of myth, and some customs and traditions have sprouted in its short history, but it leaves its patients to develop further or live within their already existing cultures. It can free from certain neurotic chains, but it cannot create and constitute the warmth and intensity of the surrounding world we seem to need. The emphasis on introspection as an analytic tool, and then a lifetime hygienic habit, leads toward separateness, isolation. It is the further work of the analysand to find her/his way back into a common humanity, to find ways to become the communal animal we most probably are. Psychoanalysis may be an introduction to culture but that's all. The wind howls in the empty corridors of psychoanalysts' homes just as it does in those of the society at large. It seems that for human beings a strong, healthy ego must commit itself to group memories, group needs, group anticipations. Like JJ Greenberg at a pro-Soviet Jewry demonstration, we are all our happiest when we are least self-conscious and most bound together with others. My analyst will understand that the problems of my communal self began after we had ended our work.

This need for tradition poses many problems for the nonaligned, nonaffiliated family. Christmas is a kind of checking point where one can stop and view oneself on the assimilation route. My mother described to me how at Christmastime she would stare at all the store windows on Upper Broadway, at the gentle, glowing lights of the Christmas tree, and how she wanted that tree in her home, bright and covered with tinsel and with sparkling cotton at the base. Her family would not consider such a thing. They didn't make much of a fuss over Channukah either because in those psychologically unsophisticated days they didn't know that they needed to comfort their children with a solstice symbol of the return of the sun as powerful as any other. My mother was uncertain whether or not to have a tree in her home when she was first married. My father was equally indifferent to the symbols of all religions and holidays did not bring any particular joy to his heart. My mother had suffered three miscarriages when I was born on December 25. The matter of the tree was decided by the German nurse. It became a family custom for all the Phillips family to come and have Christmas dinner at our house. We exchanged presents under the tree, extra ones for me because it was my birthday. My birthday cake was always decorated with red and green. My mother, who may have experienced some guilt over the first tree, threw herself into the Christmas spirit with all her unused energy. On the dining table, we had wreaths and reindeer pulling little carts. We had ice-cream molds in the shape of Santa Claus and Christmas bells. We had holly on the mantel and mistletoe hung from the chandelier.

My German nurse provided what I always considered the best part of all. Each Christmas she would make us a little village miniature on a dresser top. Cotton made the snowy hills, a pocket mirror made a lake and in Yorkville she had found little houses, miniature Bavarian chalets that were placed on the tiny hills. There were skaters on the pond and skiers down the hill and of course at the center of the village was a tiny church with its steeple rising high and outside the church there was a small manger where the baby Jesus lay. Each year she would set it up while I was sleeping and in the morning there it was and I would feel as if anything in the world were possible, that someday I might even shrink myself and join my winter village and skate on that pond and ski down that hill and go to the beautiful church on the center slope near the manger of the baby Jesus. As an adult I have tried to make such a village for my children but the ones I make look tacky, plastic, shabby and without magical possibility. I have given it up. I don't know if it is the image of the transport trains on their way to Dachau moving through the little villages of Bavaria that made it impossible for me to recreate the toy village of my childhood.

My brother, as he grew older and nearer to his Bar Mitzvah, began to take his religion seriously. He didn't like the Christmas tree. My mother felt that we were American and "Christmas," she would say, "is an American holiday." I grew up finding nothing odd about a holiday that was a Christmas without a Christ, whose spiritual significance was elusive, or perhaps it was my birthday that brought out all the red and green.

In adulthood I have taken to having friends over for Christmas. It is a sign of where one stands in the assimilation process if the people closest to you are friends rather than relatives (this is a sociological measure of Americanization in all ethnic groups). We have turkey and cranberries for dinner and there is an angel on top of our tree. For some years we have read aloud A Child's Christmas in Wales by Dylan Thomas. This reading is, I suppose, a kind of liturgy; since poetry and excellent prose are something we all honor, we are able to make the writer's artistry a substitute for the religious lacks in our celebration. We are outsiders in matters of faith but good writing is a form of faith of its own. There we feel we belong even if the subject is a Christmas scene in a country we have never been to among people we have no connections with.

Once my mother accepted a Christmas tree in the house that moved me further along the assimilation line toward the Christian mainstream, and while I still say I am Jewish, the Jewishness of my children has been so washed out as to have reached near invisibility. If I am some mongrel creature, they will have been deracinated altogether.

In fact this matters to me, not because I am so fond of the monotheism of my ancestors, not because I would want to reverse the clock and return to the shtetl. But if belief systems, culture itself, are like the child's precious blanket, a kind of transitional object that represents the union with the mother as one permits oneself to fall asleep into the darkness from which one must trust there will be an awakening, then I recognize that we need those blankets. We need (at least at this stage of evolution) to belong to tribes, to tribes with particular distinguishing marks. We need to be involved in ritual activity of some sort. We will go blind from staring directly into the bright sun of meaninglessness. We simply need those illusions Freud spoke of. There is probably some kind of ecological balance in the human psyche. We suffer if we are closed in, imprisoned, limited, but at the same time there is an intolerance for universality. We sicken without specific structures. We languish with too much freedom. We grow ugly and empty if each generation claims the world is new and the past invalid. Technology has made us universalists. Our biology, moving at its own pace, keeps us tribal as we were in the beginnings that were, after all, only a minute ago in evolutionary terms.

What is not true, and what some Jews might be tempted to believe, is that you need to be Jewish to have a deep moral position and commitment in this world. One can be ignorant of all the sayings of the wise old rabbis and still acknowledge the Magna Carta, the Declaration of Independence, the words of Rousseau, Hobbes, Emerson, the art of Leonardo da Vinci, Michelangelo and Dante, the science of Darwin, Newton and Galileo. These were not Jewish, and the great Jewish thinkers, Freud, Marx and Einstein, Claude Lévi-Strauss, studied at Christian universities and learned from Christian scholars. Jews are fond of telling you that learning is the center of Jewish culture, that the little boy learned his letters by being given alphabet-shaped bread dipped in honey so that he would learn his letters in sweetness. This may be true, but the great universities of the West were founded without Jews, the Latin scholars equal their Hebrew colleagues in scholasticism and piety. The Christian world created Oxford, Cambridge, the Sorbonne, Harvard and Yale, and Jews needed to be at least partially assimilated, free of the most intellectually limiting of their customs, in order to enter the Christian society and once there make major and special contributions. Max Brod, the Czech writer, has written a touching story of a little boy made to study long hours and forbidden the pleasures of nature and free exploration. That little boy's mind in his cheder is being stunted and deformed in ways just as crippling as was the binding of Chinese women's feet.

Now to the matter of Yiddishkeit, that elusive cultural state that was part of my heritage and not part of my life. Humor is one of the wonders of Yiddish and my brother has a section of his brain in which he has cataloged every Jewish joke in the world and at the hint of an association his synapses jump into action and he says, "That reminds me of a joke." Sometimes he has to translate it into English for me. At any rate it always sounds like it's just been translated. The warehouse of jokes he carries mostly mocks the pretensions of Jews who are pushing to deny the greenhorn status. They mock the piety of the overly religious, the Socialism of the Socialist, they prick holes into the ideal and return the truth to the nastiness of reality. The subjects of these jokes are, like Yiddish itself, passing from the scene and they will become harder and harder for future generations to understand, and yet the Jewish joke (my brother's incredible collection) reminds me that he has incorporated, ingested, an entire culture that I excluded myself from.

It is as if he lived in a foreign country, slightly backward, quaint, rich in memories and humor, and at the same time went to Columbia University, became a doctor, read Proust and Thomas Mann, took out multiple citizenships while I had only one. Unfair, but this was my own fault. Yiddishkeit gave my brother comfort from which he drew a sense of himself and gained strength. Yiddishkeit was not much in evidence at the golf and tennis club my parents belonged to. It was just under the surface but not visible. It was not in the German nurse or the Irish maid or the black washerwoman. Since Yiddishkeit could belong to a Socialist, a Marxist, a nonconformist, it gave one a way to be Jewish without being religious. One could be Jewish to the core if your parents read the *Forward*, because you spoke Yiddish, because their memories of the old country were told to you, because you lived among Jews who still remembered the old country, because you were the object of anti-Semitism. My brother made a special journey to distant parts of this city to find his Yiddishness and when he brought it home I reacted a little as I do now when the cat presents us with one of her dead mice on the doorstep. Now that the assimilation parade has moved on, it will be difficult if not impossible for a new generation to be Jewish through this Yiddishkeit. It would be like trying to be a Pompeian by pitching a tent outside New York's Museum of Natural History during its show on Pompeii. The best of imaginations would be diverted by the activity on Central Park West.

My brother can only give to his son some reflection of what he has, and that may be forgotten or certainly thinned out by the other strong cultural influences that will affect the child.

If Darth Vader blurs into Hitler and the fate of the Empire
grows as important in his mind as the State of Israel, who
knows how his Jewish identity will look?

As the religious Jew daily reaffirms his faith, so I now
check about my unconscious, rummaging like a bag lady in the
unconscious. I have to ask myself whether writing this book
is not itself a provocation to ask the Certain Ones (whose
answers never change shape with changes in wind or climate)
to attack. Am I, on the other hand, writing to apologize to
some unknown mythical grandparent, a loving fantasy of
whom may lurk in my unconscious? Am I, out of perversity,
trying to put into words things that should not be said to the
goyim? It is probable that I am looking for Mama in the
mama-loshen or Daddy in the line of patriarchs, the authority
of the rabbis. Am I just weary of trying to figure everything
out on my own? Am I trying to find a way to abandon personal
responsibility by hiding within a group life?

What, then, is wrong with this assimilation? There must be
something wrong if I am willing to suffer the pity of Blu
Greenberg and not fight back. I have, after all, certain advan-
tages. I don't think of the world in terms of Jewish or non-
Jewish, and I'm sure that helps in thinking about the world.
I am not under the yoke of taboos that limit my selection of
food, sex or marriage partners. I do not feel the temptation to
value the life of an Eastern European Jew over that of an
Arab or Cambodian. I do not need to be surrounded by Jews.
I can move freely through many classes of American society.
But I suffer a depression I cannot ignore. One that is not part
of my private psychological baggage but springs from sources
beyond the reach of psychoanalysis, the interstices of communal life. It is simply not easy to live cut off from the past
and without a cushion of symbolic acts and occasions that bind
into the particular and reinforce the self. I feel vulnerable to
an unease that the constant reading of modern literature only
confirms and inflames but does not release me from. I am certain that the promise of Americanization made to my father

and my husband's father has gone sour. Is it because of materialism? Is it because it happened too quickly? I don't feel a real part of this nation because at bottom I am a Jew. After Germany only in Israel can a Jew feel really connected and I am not enough of a Jew to go to Israel. In Israel now I would be odd even among other odd people. It is interesting to note that the writers of the upper-middle-class Jewish experience, Erica Jong, Lois Gould, and others, are mainly women. Is it possible that you needed the toughness of a woman to survive the emotional assault of middle-class Jewish life?

I cannot literally believe in the coming of the Messiah, but living with the knowledge that the birth of a child or one's own death is an end in itself, not part of a process with meaning and history, is sad. If everything is random, accidental and disordered, and the wise man is not the mystic who sees the harmony and balance of things but rather the one who stares unflinching at the accidental motions of chemicals, then in such a lonely, grim landscape, how can anyone proceed with work or pleasure? Why begin? Why continue? Where and how to take courage? How diminished is the private self when one has amputated the support of ancient tribe and its communal destiny. It is true that I, ex-bohemian, beatnik, Leftist, also need ceremonies to mark the marriages of my children, to mark the burials, initiations, transitions, to shape the seasons of the year, to grant a specific time to rest and appreciate those around us. Listening to the Greenbergs and the Solomans describe their Sabbath, I recognize my own attempts to separate the special from the mundane. If I wrote a long letter to a child from the tooth fairy, if I had everyone at the Christmas breakfast table make a wish for someone else, if I spent hours baking birthday cakes and tying balloons to light fixtures, then I was trying to mark off special time. The traditional Jewish way of doing things would have satisfied and gratified those largely unmet needs. Even in Auschwitz the sense of Jewishness, the celebration in whatever way possible of the Jewish holidays, sustained Anna Ornstein and others. Of course there is something dreary and offensive about suggesting that life within the Jewish nation should be lived because it is good for your mental health. It won't work that way. Some new mental-health fad will come to take its place. Jewishness cannot be a form of Valium, an Alcoholics Anonymous, a lifetime membership in an est community. It is a comment on the bleakness of our times that I have almost come to the point of making just such a suggestion.

From the humblest tailor in the shtetl to the court Jews, from Tevye to Kissinger, from Chasid to Maskil, from Rothschild to Marx, there have been errors in the Jewish way. The suffocating of women, the taboos that clouded sexuality and made one dislike the body—these have been Jewish cruelties. But taken all together the nationhood is a landscape of incredible grandeur, and the culture itself, the more one knows of it, well, the more it shines with radiance.

I now regret my ignorance of the languages, I regret my ignorance of the customs. I regret the meagerness of the knowledge that I have and I hold on tightly both to the sense of being Jewish and to the rest of the world that I have learned to live in, including the art of Crete and the poems of the seventeenth-century English. I want now the richness of the particular Jewish life and the universality, the political and artistic knowledge of the world in general. There are obvious difficulties with this greediness.

Being a secular human appears not to affect the moral sense at all. The concern and kindness, the sense of right and wrong and the ability to distinguish between them, do not depend on belief in a higher order. We know that people without conviction that their actions will be either rewarded or punished in the hereafter can behave with goodness and mercy. Even convinced of the meaninglessness of life people maintain and elaborate private moral codes. It seems to be a part of the beast—independent of a religious structure. (Perhaps Freud should have described a goodness instinct.) The great religions may have taught a basic morality but many of their adherents don't practice it and many of their defectors do. Organized religion has such a shoddy record of misalliances that religious authorities are among the most mistrusted of mortals.

But when I think of our traditions of the family, traditions that are eclectic, thin, without magic or the density of time, I can see that we have made an error. I appreciate our Thanksgiving and Christmas. I know that I will make beautiful weddings for our daughters and that our funerals will serve well enough. But I do believe that the tensions of the ancient ways, the closeness to primitive magic, the patina of the ages and the sense of connection to past and future that are lacking in our lives are serious losses. Our morality is only as tarnished as most earth creatures' by our style of living in which we celebrate no ancient victories, in which we atone for nothing and are thankful for little, in which we have no group cultural past and no group cultural future—this is not adequate.

Had I been educated like Samuel and Rhoda Soloman, I would not have moved so far into the secular world. I would, of course, be someone else. I believe on balance that the well-being and happiness of my family would have been better supported within the wealth of a Jewish past. If I had had a deeper Jewish education I could return to it now (and fight for the betterment of the position of women within it). As it is, our universalism, once my joy, my breakthrough toward freedom, becomes my burden.

While I don't like the idea of being a parvenue or a pariah, that condition will be washed away with time, as the generations follow each other. The assimilated family in the future will have forged a new kind of authenticity, and certainly whatever that place is, they will eventually arrive. But will they join other tribes or will they be so universal, such citizens of the world, that they will be bland, ineffectual, gracious but ridiculous, like the meetings of the United Nations? In their universalism will the furnishings of their souls look like Olympic stadiums? The idea makes me anxious for my children.

Politics are an important necessity for the Jew. I don't just mean pro-Israel politics, or anti-Soviet politics. I mean the kind of moral political activity for the oppressed and silenced of the world that involves some sacrifices of personal comfort, that translates one's moral positions into some kind of action. The Judaism of the middle-class Jews, who found themselves increasingly comfortable and increasingly less willing to take risks for other people, is not a Judaism that can expect renewed vigor. JJ Greenberg, all the Greenberg family, Samuel and Rhoda Soloman, do not live as consumers. They have placed themselves at the service of the causes and political actions that are most important to them. Without this political activism they too might be mere hypocrites. Their ability to act, to do something for others, binds them deeper and deeper into the line of their people and on every level enriches their lives. My mother used to say as we drove through the Bronx, "I wish we had a candy store that I ran with your father. I think that would make me happy." My father was always infuriated by this remark. He regarded it as romantic and stupid. My mother wished she was poor and had something to do that made her days seem full and necessary. She was wishing she had a function for her hands and her mind and dimly she must have guessed that the family had paid too high a price for their share of the material comforts of the world.

A Judaism that does not involve new commitments, work for others, will melt away in the heat of the barbecue on the patio, the light of the TV, the warmth of the variety of comforts now available. Reform Judaism has been the easy way out for a generation of comfortable, nearly assimilated Jews. In many affluent communities it somehow has often lost the mystery and drama, the terror of the burning bush, the excitement in the bondage or the covenant. If one modernizes Judaism too far it becomes like a TV game show as compared to a fine Shakespeare performance (a Doris Day film as compared to a Fellini or Bergman). Indifferently the next generation is tempted to drift away, to turn it off.

Returning to the Jewish body is made complicated by the question of the Jewish God. Religion without God is precarious if not foolish. It is possible in rhetoric but I'm not sure if it can work in fact. Richard L. Rubenstein, distinguished professor of the Department of Religion, Florida State University, says, "I believe the greatest single challenge to modern Judaism arises out of the question of God and the death camps. Though I believe that a void stands where once we experienced God's presence, I do not think Judaism has lost its meaning or its power. I do not believe that a theistic God is necessary for Jewish life. We no longer believe in a God who has the power to annul the tragic necessities of existence; the need religiously to share that existence remains."

This is an exciting idea. It might make it possible for this assimilated Jew to grope back to her nation and live there. But the mind does boggle at the specifics of the route. If the same prayers are to be repeated they now become mockeries. If they are not repeated the forms of the religion are lost. If Jewish history is taught without the emphasis on the redemption and the coming of the Messiah, what gives the Jewish nation its purpose, its cohesion? If Judaism is taught to the children without pressing a faith in God, then new traditions and rituals and forms will have to develop because to repeat the old ones won't work. The Kiddush, the blowing of the shofar, the minyan, the calling to Torah, the High Holidays, these will become dead forms without some incredible ingenuity. To repeat these old forms but tell the next generation they are only symbolic or partial truths, are relics of another age and an old way of looking at things, is to invite a washing away of Judaism such as occurred in the Park Avenue Synagogue of my childhood and in Reform synagogues throughout this country. Perhaps there are solutions to be found.

Emil L. Fackenheim, the well-known Jewish theologian, in *God's Presence in History* (New York: New York University

Press, 1970), has written, "What does the voice of Auschwitz command? Jews are forbidden to hand Hitler posthumous victories. They are comanded to survive as Jews, lest the Jewish people perish. They are forbidden to despair of man and his world, and to escape into either cynicism or other-worldliness, lest they cooperate in delivering the world over to the forces of Auschwitz. Finally they are forbidden to despair of the God of Israel, lest Judaism perish. A secularist Jew cannot make himself believe by a mere act of will nor can he be commanded to do so. And a religious Jew who has stayed with his God may not be forced into new revolutionary relationships with Him. One possibility, however, is wholly unthinkable. A Jew may not respond to Hitler's attempt to destroy Judaism by himself cooperating in its destruction. In ancient times the unthinkable Jewish sin was idolatry. Today it is to respond to Hitler by doing his work."

But how can secular Jews avoid handing Hitler this victory if not in their own lifetime then in the lifetime of their children? Jewishness cannot (unless another Hitler arises) survive merely as a secular affinity, a memory of what other generations believed or were like. While the Jewish nation exists today independent of whether God designed it or it designed God, this cannot continue without some life-enhancing experience within each generation that will pass it on to the next, who must also find its forms enriching, and gratifying. Without that the extreme end of the assimilation parade will continue to carry off Jews to universalism, odd cults, political fanaticisms, and in boredom and indifference the nation will dwindle and Hitler and the new Hitlers will be handed victories every day.

Rabbi Greenberg has said there may be a new covenant written between man and God. He has said that women in the new covenant may take on an equal role with men. He has said that perhaps a dialectical process is possible where one can doubt and believe at the same time. He describes it this way:

217

"Thus if the Holocaust strikes at the credibility of faith, especially reconstructed faith, then dialectically it also erodes the persuasiveness of the secular opposition." Greenberg argues: "The Holocaust calls on Jew, Christian, and others to absolutely resist the total authority of this cultural moment—the rehabilitation of one-half million survivors in Israel speaks of the reclamation of tremendous human dignity and value. If Treblinka makes human hope an illusion, then the Western Wall asserts that human dreams are more real than force and facts. Israel's faith in the God of History demands that an unprecedented event of destruction be matched by an unprecedented act of redemption and this has happened." It is perhaps an ironic and tribal truth that one group's redemption created the exodus and the Diaspora of another, and the favor of the God of History was the absence and silence of another God of History. If Israel is destroyed, whether through its own intransigence or through forces completely beyond control, what then becomes of this fickle God of History?

Rabbi Greenberg's dialectical religion, which would permit moments of doubt (he believes this is a time to doubt) along with moments of faith, seems at least a starting point. It needs thinking about. I wonder what kind of Jewish religion he would design if asked. I wonder how he would save the old forms but imbue them with meaning even for an age of doubt. I wonder if my mind has become too modern or too secular to try. I would try and I would want my children to try. Perhaps some imaginative ways can be found.

Perhaps there is a kind of Reform Judaism that exists or can be created that would be: (1) Serious and genuinely intellectual (not a version of Judaism to please golf players in suburbia). (2) Political (JJ Greenberg's Judaism), that is to say in active opposition to human suffering of all kinds, in active relation to not just Soviet Jews but Cambodians, Afghans, blacks, and others. (3) A Judaism that creates a new emphasis on the heroic Judaic tradition and not the lachrymose one. It must not engender a sense of helplessness or victim mentality. (4) Liberal, tolerant, unafraid of or threatened by other Jews' ways of doing things or other people's. (5) Deeply tribal but without the exclusivity, the snobbism, the clannishness that deprives one of the outside world. Is this an impossible paradox? There are probably many Jewish groups trying to achieve this right now whom I don't know. Perhaps good starts have been made by people I have not yet met. But I wonder can even Rabbi Greenberg find a way to be close within one nation without being narrow and exclusive? Intellectually able to maintain a dialogue with all the major spiritual contributors of our time, to be universal without losing the pleasures of the particular? (6) Can there be a truly nonpatriarchal Judaism? Can the new attitudes toward women be infused into the centuries of prejudice? It is in the Jewish tradition for the Jewish tradition to change, so perhaps! Is it possible to find a Reform Judaism that doesn't erode before the materialism and mediocrity of this country?

I will start looking for this kind of Judaism.

July 12

WASHINGTON, CONNECTICUT

Today the Congregational church is holding its summer fair. There are large striped tents on the green and tables set up everywhere. There are flowers and plants being sold at one end and at the other are items for auction: Royal Doulton plates, silver trays, pewter vases, candy dishes, lace tablecloths and crystal glasses, an old spinning wheel and prints from the Audubon Society. There is a table under the tent where hand-knit hats and mittens are being sold along with homemade aprons and children's dresses. The ladies of the church sit behind the tables. Many of them are white-haired and wear flowered silk dresses. One looks 106 years old and calls me "dear." They make change for me as I purchase a set of gingham napkins, a stuffed horse sewn with a red plaid fabric. On one side a man is making doughnuts in a tub of deep fat. A roving clown will make up the children's faces for ten cents.

I hear crickets chirping on the grass by the large maple tree at the far corner of the green. On the porch of the church a bake sale is proceeding and in the parish house are books, rows and rows of books, for ten cents and twenty-five cents each. Browsers and buyers move up and down the aisles between the tables, greeting each other, showing off their fair treasures, inquiring after each other's relatives. The day is hot. We sit on the church steps and admire the white clapboard New England houses that surround the green, their freshly painted black shutters, their perfect white picket fences that enclose in uniformity even the post office and the drugstore. Someone tells us that last night the tent lines were cut by vandals and in the morning when the people of the church came to set up the fair they found the tents had tumbled down. Who had cut the tent lines? Some miserable adolescent probably, who hated the decorous and the conventional, who hated the appearances of propriety; messing up church fairs must be the country form of graffiti. There is a snake in everybody's paradise and malcontents among the teacups.

I reach into my brown bag of newly purchased books. I pull out Henry Roth's *Call It Sleep*. I have also found a copy of Bernard Malamud's *The Magic Barrel*. I am glad to find them among the boxes of books in the parish house. We belong here with them. Maybe we can be a part of both Jewish and secular worlds. Maybe we can find a golden mean between traditional and universalist stances. Reconciliations are possible. One of my children is rummaging through a bag of secondhand toys, another is fiddling with the hinges on a wooden card file box she has just purchased. My husband is waiting to see if he can get a 1902 collection of Blake's illustrations of the Book of Job. I hold on to my books. I belong to them and nothing will part us again.

———

ABOUT THE AUTHOR

Anne Roiphe is a novelist and journalist. Her novels include *Digging Out* (Anne Richardson), *Up the Sandbox, Long Division, Torch Song,* and *Lovingkindness*. She lives with her family in New York City.

- Strong commitment to certain traditions, but resist precise labeling.

- parvenus

- Repression of female aspiration.

- Monster of violent prejudice reappears.

- Admitting to a mystical, suprarational connection.

(Freud: obscure emotional forces, clear consciousness of inner identity safe privacy of a common mental construct

- "I care that the Jewishness Continues"

Has a Tradition that must have been rife with human effort to simply die off?